The Greatest Guide to
Life
Coaching

Printed and bound in the United Kingdom

ISBN 978-1-907906-09-1

I would like to dedicate this book with love to my daughters Danielle and Christine

Contents

A few words from Simone…

Wouldn't it be great if there was someone helping you to get right to the heart of what you really want and encouraging you to take steps to make positive lasting change? Life Coaching is now the most popular way to help people to really take charge of their lives, creating life goals that bring the happiness they so much desire.

This book is written for anyone who wants to feel happy and fulfilled in their life and whether they are at a crossroads in their life and need to make a big decision or simply doubt what to do next, then they will find inspiration and practical techniques and tools within this book to release their potential, increase their motivation, develop more confidence and create the personal happiness they truly want.

I hope you enjoy the tips in this book and if you only apply some of them to your life, you will be creating a positive change. Remember, obstacles are those frightening things you see when you take your eyes of the goal, so read on, find your passion, challenge yourself, set your life goals and take action.

Simone x

One life…

One life, one smile,
many chances for a while.
Once swift and with haste,
time and laughter with no grace.

Work, family and health,
invisible growth and stealth.
Years follow on, questions arise
recalling love and loss demise.

Performing life for another,
a single sheep behind it's mother.
Commit and aim, be your best –
stumble, strive, push on with zest.

Life and grace does not wait
for those who watch dry paint
Look up, climb high, don't be afraid to fall.
Make every moment count, get over that wall.

One life, one smile,
many chances for a while.
Be swift, be hasty
for life is sweet and very tasty.

By Simone Ryder

What is Life Coaching?

" The past does not equal the future. "

Anon

Chapter 1
What is Life Coaching?

Many people are drawn to life coaching because they feel their life is out of balance. They may be working too hard and have no time left for all the other things they value or they may be going through a big change – in their relationship, career, family, money, health or home – all of which have an unbalancing effect and create fears and feelings of uncertainty. Life coaching helps people to know themselves what they really want and how to move forward; from this point they can then make decisions with confidence.

Life Coaching originated in the United States and developed out of sport and business coaching, whereby a trained coach would help their sporting athlete or business client to set specific goals and then work alongside them to motivate, encourage and support them to success, using various techniques and motivational tools to help them gain progress. The coach would also help their client break past any negative beliefs that they may have about their ability, which might be holding them back.

It's not just about goals – it's taking action

Using a life coach helps you to structure your daily thoughts into a routine, set goals and act daily to achieve them and with a clear agenda, it transforms your mindset and habits into positive action.

What's your attitude?

If you use a life coach to help you set your new agenda for the life you want, then clear and powerful revelations will take place. Negative thought patterns are worked through and eliminated and positive empowering thoughts are created in order for you to quite simply see the wood for the trees. This will help you to look at your attitude to yourself, your life, your capabilities and what you really want. Adjusting your mindset to a positive *can do* attitude.

Who needs a life coach?

Many people think life coaching is like a form of counseling or therapy, an opportunity to sit and pour out your problems. However, although life coaching has similarities with therapy, such as listening and helping a person in a non-judgemental and confidential environment, its main objective is to help people know who they are and what they want for their life, help them be true to themselves and take action to change their life in a positive way, with the focus on *taking action* and motivating the person to move forward.

Focus and breaking through

As with counseling, a life coach will listen and empathize with their client to help them have clarity on their life situation and this will include looking at the issues, behavior and feelings around the client's current life. However, the life coach will help the client to look beyond this and help them set personal goals, motivate, inspire and encourage their client to move forward into the life they would like, whilst looking at the impact of any changes they make to all the areas of their life, breaking through old patterns of behavior and limiting beliefs that may cause them to feel stuck.

Life coaching may feel a little like a therapy session at times, however, the client should come away with a clear set of actions and should feel motivated to achieve them. Over a period of time the coach will challenge the client to move forward in achieving their goals step by step.

Life coach, mentor, therapist or counselor?

Mentors

These people are usually experts in their particular area or job and have lots of experience to help other people in the same field. They will help by listening and then advising and guiding another person over a period of time. An example of this might be a tutor with a student or a senior manager with a new salesperson on their team.

Therapists

There are many types of therapist: sport therapist, art therapist, dance therapist, psychotherapist. A therapist is usually medically trained in their particular field and is skilled at treating emotional or psychological disorders. Another example of this might be a branch of therapy such as hypnotherapy whereby a person will be helped with specific issues, phobias or addictions such as wanting to stop smoking.

Counselors

Work with people to help them explore a difficulty, feelings of distress, or dissatisfaction in their life. They provide a safe environment, listening to and encouraging clients to think clearly about their situation and perhaps consider a new perspective. Counselors do not give advice or direct a client to a solution, but help the client to choose freely a way forward by reducing confusion and promoting a better understanding of themselves.

Life Coaches

These are upbeat, positive people who work to get the very best out of someone enabling them to make decisions that will improve their life. Coaches help people to move forward and do not claim to have all the answers. A coach's job is to understand and empathize with their client, which includes understanding the client's background, and then they work with the client to help them find the answers within themselves. This can cover a number of areas, for example: achieving a better work/life balance; feeling more fulfilled at work; improving relationships with family and partners; learning better parenting skills that benefit both the child and parent; gaining a spiritual meaning to life, or a desire to 'get sorted'.

It's a relationship dedicated to you

A life coach is more of a partnership than anything else. It is a support system with one goal in mind: improving your quality of life. Time that you dedicate specifically to yourself to improve your life and your happiness. In order for coaching to work, it takes courage for the person being coached to be totally honest about who they are and what they really want from life, sometimes people don't even know what they want! It takes a skilled coach to help their client feel they can be open and honest with themselves first, enabling their client to feel relaxed and respected to be themselves, without judgement.

What do you want?

A life coach will direct this question to their client in many ways and encourage their client to think hard and deeply about what is most important to them. For many people this is the first time they have been able to be completely honest about what they truly want and as they look at each area of their life, they begin to see patterns of behavior and experiences that have developed out of not really knowing what they want and following a vague idea of what being happy means to them. Many people have never taken the time to understand who they are and what they value most in life, considering 'being happy' as enough. However, being happy means very different things to people and when this is looked at more closely the coach can usually see very clearly what the client needs to do or change in order to have a happy life. It is important to point out here that a life coach does not tell their client what they think; they help the client to find out what they really want by asking probing questions and giving feedback to ensure the client understands what is being said, as this is the only way the client can be truly sure it is they who have discovered what they really want and not a suggestion from someone else. The difficult part for many is getting past the fears that have kept them from making the positive changes already!

What makes a good life coach?

Firstly, training qualifications from a reputable training organization and a variety of technical coaching skills such as NLP (Neuro Linguistic Programming, explained below) can have a beneficial effect in helping the coach to help their clients change negative patterns of behavior and limiting beliefs about themselves. Secondly a life coach who has many hours of experience in coaching people, even better if the coach has experienced positive and lasting changes in their own life due to the influence of Life Coaching themselves. They need to be authentic and open hearted about themselves in order for others to trust them.

A good life coach is definitely one who *walks the talk* which is a real strength in a life coach, as they need the ability to really empathize with other people, so the more life experience the life coach has the more they can understand the needs of their clients. Good life coaches are happy, healthy and good to be around. They may also specialize in a certain area, for example parenting skills, well-being, relocation, retirement or spiritual coaching. Life coaches who have personal experience of achieving success in their specialist areas tend to be more passionate, enthusiastic and able to help others achieve the same results.

Finding the right life coach for you

The best way to hire a great life coach is through recommendation from someone you know and then you can actually see the living proof from the success of the coaching they received. However, if you need to start from scratch in choosing a life coach, researching the internet for a life coach in your area is a good place to start; line up at least three or four and give them a call for a chat or arrange to meet them face to face if you can. A good life coach will be happy to do this and understand your need to talk or meet them first; these initial meetings are usually free of charge and informal. If your coach has not come with a recommendation, then ask the life coach to show you their qualifications and testimonials from previous clients and ask them how many coaching hours they have done with clients.

Asking questions – choosing with confidence

The best way to judge whether you will be able to get on and trust this person as your life coach is to ask them questions about who they have coached before and what successes they have had. Explain a little about your need to have a life coach and ask how they would be able to help you; ask if you can call a couple of their past clients for a recommendation and this will give you more confidence in choosing. It's also worth pointing out that we all have different personalities, so find a coach who you feel really empathizes with you and makes you feel comfortable about being yourself and yet with enough assertiveness to challenge you too!

What techniques do life coaches use?

Mainly experience and personality, however, life coaches are trained to use different tools and techniques to help you identify your goals, help you to look at what you value and how your beliefs can influence how you feel about your abilities and choices in life. The various techniques used help the coach to get inside your thoughts and find out where your thoughts are coming from; from this point they are more able to ask the right questions in order to help you see exactly who you are and why you think the way you do about your life. This is a very important part of life coaching, because it is from this point that the client can become clear about making decisions and begin to move forward.

NLP (Neuro Linguistic Programming) is a technique used by some life coaches and is believed to bring about change by taking back the control of one's own mind. We all hold negative thoughts and beliefs that have come from our past experiences, for some people these thoughts can get stuck in a pattern and feel overwhelming to change. NLP is done by applying three principles:

Neuro – the nervous system which processes and codes information into our memory.

Linguistic – the language pattern of the individual and how we communicate on a verbal level with other people or with the use of symbols such as writing words, numbers or drawings, and the neural processes of the mind.

Programming – this is the coding arrangement of the two previous elements which provides us with the means to put in order our sensors, such as our sight, smell, touch, hearing, and verbal to create new and successful behavior patterns.

" A belief is a preconceived attitude based on the past. "

Richard Wilkins

Blended coaching

Many people with existing skills of working with others are now becoming trained in coaching skills and techniques to enhance their ability to bring out the best in themselves and others. Many life coaches often use their life experience to focus on a specific field of coaching in which they have had personal experiences, such as Parent coaching, Stress Management Coaching, Health and Weight Loss Coaching. However, more and more professionals and highly trained individuals in other jobs now benefit from gaining coaching skills. These skills are blended together and provide very useful tools and techniques to bring out the best in their work environment, personal work performance and enhance the success of those they help through the course of their work already.

Teachers, Doctors and Police are just a few examples where extra coaching skills blended together with key work skills increase the benefit to those they have to communicate with and work to help.

The power of music

A certain piece of music can put you straight into a good mood. The brain will remember how you felt happy when you heard that music and experienced something happy in the past. The same is true of sad experiences. Music is very powerful at influencing our feelings fast, so next time you want to feel positive and upbeat, but on your favorite piece of music and notice how the brain immediately changes state.

How does this NLP work in coaching?

It's all about creating winning patterns in the mind, which produce positive habits and patterns of behavior. NLP takes the old patterns (which may have been negative and self doubting) and creates new patterns, which gives the person more control over how they feel and see their world and their abilities.

Therefore, life coaches who have trained in NLP to become practitioners, will use their knowledge gained from understanding the principles of NLP to help them understand their clients more deeply; they are able to use these techniques to benefit their clients in getting past limiting beliefs and help them to break through old patterns when they have felt blocked and unable to change the way they think.

NLP provides a different perspective on the expression of life – for example some of the expressions a coach may use when they want to get their client to think about making positive changes:

1. If what you are doing is not working, do something else.

2. People already have all the resources they need inside their minds.

3. The meaning of your communication is the response that you get.

4. The mind and the body are parts of the same system.

5. People always make the best choices available to them.

One person's experience of NLP...

To give you just one simple example of how NLP works: a lady had wanted to lose weight for several years and talked about it a lot, tried various diets and genuinely did not like feeling overweight and unhealthy. She caught a glance of herself in a grocery store window and felt shocked that she looked that way, as she felt she was a different person on the outside from how she felt she looked on the inside. The lady decided to get fit and stop eating junk food, she had over 50 pounds to lose and so she talked to a life coach about why she wanted to do this. She wanted to have more energy, feel more confident and live longer, and yet during her coaching sessions she discovered that her mind had built a pattern of thinking about food that was attached to her emotions and this had supported her overeating with a negative perception of herself. These feelings were reinforced in the negative way she spoke about herself and this negative belief was stopping her from achieving the success she so wanted in losing weight.

Every time she was ready to lose weight and was totally committed to it, the old feelings of inadequacy and that she didn't deserve to be happy (slim and fit) came creeping back and sabotaged her good intentions. The lady had not realized that she had been programming her mind and body over many years to accept the negative thoughts she had about herself and the overeating helped her to ignore these bad feelings and comfort the sadness they generated.

Using NLP she looked more deeply into why she had been overeating and why she had tried and failed many times to stop and lose the weight. It soon became clear to her that she had formed a limiting belief about herself and had become afraid of being her true self; the real her which was slim, confident and in control of her life had been pushed out of her mind with all the negative thoughts and so NLP and her coach began to replace the negative with the truth and the real feelings of happiness came back and began to motivate and inspire her to succeed. This lady began to realize that past experiences which had knocked her confidence, had set up a negative pattern (programme) in her subconscious about her self-worth, which she had accepted as the truth!

With her new insight this lady was then able to replace the old pattern of thinking with the one she wanted to experience. Using visualization to see and experience her life as a success, part of which was losing the weight and getting fit, the lady then started with realistic steps to achieve her goals, keeping her new belief clear in her mind. She went on to lose all the weight and tell her story in this book!

This lady is me, Simone the author. Not only did I lose the weight but I also identified the life I truly wanted to live, the sort of relationships I wanted with my children and wider family, the job I wanted to do, the place I wanted to live, the things I wanted to experience and once this was clear in my mind and I accepted that only I could make my life a success, I moved forward slowly, step by step changing these things for the better and creating the life I wanted.

Finding my life purpose

Brenda had reached a point in her life where her children were grown up and moving on and she spent her days wondering what to do with her time and worrying about what her children were doing, focusing on them instead of herself. Her identity had been so tightly combined with being a mother all those years and putting the needs of her family first, that she just about managed to fit in the odd bit of time for herself, sound familiar?

Brenda was happy to be a Mom through all those years, but now the nest felt empty and her sense of purpose was gone. We worked together to identify all her values and bring them to her awareness. This helped her to see how many things were very important to her beyond her family, not to mention her talents.

Once the focus for Brenda had turned from who she had been, to who she wanted to be and what would make her happy, the biggest challenge was for her to choose what she would like to do and then allow herself the permission to go for it. Going through a change in life like children growing up really pulls on the heart and moving on with your own life often feels strange. Once a mother, always a mother. When Brenda realized it was not letting go of who she was as a mother, but more about embracing opportunities and becoming even more of who she was, then the steps forward were easier.

I know what this feels like myself, my daughters as I write this book are 23 and 17. I had dedicated my life to being there for them and putting them first. It was a struggle to 'find myself' when they didn't need me as much, and I was reluctant to look at my life without motherhood being my main role and to be honest my main motivation to get up in the mornings sometimes too. However, coaching does help you to see beyond the present and ask yourself honest questions about what YOU would like and thank goodness I did – I am always going to be a Mom, but my work helping others is my purpose!

Summary

- A great life coach is passionate about life and is someone who inspires you and 'walks the talk'.

- When you have life coaching, focusing on what you value will help you to understand what is most important to you and your life.

- Coaching may appear to be like therapy sometimes, but you should come away with clearly defined goals, motivation, and a plan of action.

- Time with your coach is about you taking 100% responsibility for improving your life and personal happiness.

- Setting goals for your life is one of the most liberating and exciting things you can do to improve it.

- Discovering the patterns of your behavior and how they may limit your personal success and confidence is revealed to you through life coaching.

- Clarify your 'purpose in life' through coaching and you will find that your passion and motivation for life will increase.

- Ideally get a recommendation for a great coach, alternatively line up three or four coaches to talk to before you choose your personal coach.

- Personality and an ability to empathize with you is necessary for a good life coach to understand what you need and want, and then help you move forward.

- NLP techniques are a way to help you overcome limiting patterns of behavior that may be stopping you from achieving personal success; visualization is one element of NLP.

Embracing Change

" *Change a <u>can't</u> to a <u>could</u> and you've got a <u>chance</u>.* **"**

Anon

Chapter 2
Embracing Change

One thing we can all be sure of is that life will keep presenting us with challenges and our lives will go through a continual cycle of change. However, most people don't enjoy too much change, it upsets the flow of life and generally we like to know that things are the same from one day to the next; it gives us a sense of security and continuity in our lives. So it's no surprise that when we have to face some difficult challenges in life and changes that come along from time to time, it can cause us to feel insecure and out of control and we really don't like the feeling of too much uncertainty.

Some changes we choose and in doing so inflict a sense of unease and uncertainty in our lives, because it excites us and we feel it will be a good or great change with all the feelings that will come with it: getting married is a good example!

However, there are many things that come as a shock to our lives too, and when change is unplanned it can be derailing for our emotions and can take time for us to adjust.

Let's take a look at just some of the areas in life that create challenge for us and the changes we have to adapt to.

1. Moving to a new home.

2. Getting engaged or married.

3. Getting divorced or splitting with a long term partner!

4. Having a baby or becoming a step-parent.

5. Starting in a new job.

6. Dating again after divorce.

7. New systems or new boss at work.

8. Becoming unemployed.

9. 40th birthday or any other birthday for that matter!

10. Living in a different country.

11. Bringing up a young family.

12. Getting and looking older!

13. Health problems.

14. Looking after elderly parents.

15. Losing someone close.

16. Retirement.

17. Meeting the love of your life!

18. Winning the lottery!

19. Grown up kids leaving the home (nest).

20. Starting your own business.

Wow! The list is endless, but the reality is that we are challenged daily with change; sometimes it is out of choice and we want that change and know it will be a challenge but it feels positive. However, other times change is thrust upon us or even creeps up without us seeing it and – bang! – it feels like such a shock and so unexpected, it can really upset the balance of our life.

Interestingly, we sometimes even know that change is going to happen, good or bad and yet we don't face how we feel about it until we absolutely have no choice, which is usually when it has a definite effect on our emotions, health or behavior. The people who seem so positive in life are generally those that have had to learn to adapt to change as fast as possible so that they can get on and live their lives. In fact we all know of people who have been through tremendous suffering and yet they are the ones that are often most positive – why is that we ask? It's because they have learnt that through suffering, accepting and finding a new way forward makes us stronger and more able to cope with what life hits us with. You can guarantee life is full of unexpected surprises that knock us down and we have to find a way back to balance if we are to be happy.

Becoming aware of the change

Once you know something has changed in your life it can throw you into a state of shock to start with and for some time it might be difficult to make sense of what has happened. If you have gone through this, take a moment to think about a time when something changed in your life and the feelings you went through until you adjusted to the change.

Many people feel a sense of shock and then a mixture of feelings depending on what the change is. The key to moving through change and coping with it effectively is to first be aware of what is happening and allow the feelings to be acknowledged, then move forward into finding a way out of any negative feelings into a more positive state.

Now write down what changes you are going through in your life today and how this is challenging you:

. . . .
. . . .
. . . .
. . . .
. . . .
. . . .
. . . .

First steps to change

The first steps to coping with change is acknowledging what is happening and how you honestly feel about it. So let's take a look at your challenges and what has changed or is changing in your life that you want to focus on. I now want you to acknowledge how you really feel about it. It will help you to write these feelings down in your notes or circle the words below that you think describe how you feel. Don't be surprised if you feel a mixture of positive and negative feelings all together!

Scared	Worried	Excited	Angry	Resentful
Lonely	Depressed	Sad	Confused	Insecure
Happy	Secure	Anxious	Restless	Calm
Quiet	Out of control	Relaxed	Motivated	Enthusiastic
Lost	Confident	Stressed	Positive	Negative

OK great – so take a look at what you have acknowledged and accept that this is how you feel and that whatever it is, this is the real you right now. The next question that always comes up in life coaching: What are you going to do about it? Do you want to stay like this or do you want it to change? And if you want it to change then this is the point at which you can honestly start to look at your options of how to move forward into feeling more positive and in control again.

Moving on through change

If change is something we can't stop, then learning to live with change and accepting that it will keep happening will help us to move with change quicker and adjust in order to find happiness and balance in our lives again. For some people, they hold onto how they wanted their life to be before a big change came along and feel unable to move forward. For others, it may feel somehow that moving on will mean letting go of a certain level of control they feel in hanging on to the past, however this is a false belief and whilst they are busy looking backwards at the old times they are missing out on their future. This is hard to do sometimes when the future may look uncertain with further changes! When you feel like this, the feelings you circled above are what will be holding you back.

The truth is that when you have something that makes you happy and secure you want to hold on to that, it makes sense for us not to want to cause difficulty in our lives. However, when change comes along and it means letting go of this, then the more important this security is – whether it be a job, a person, a home, an age – the more you don't want to lose it. But ask yourself "Do I really have what I had before?". Admit to yourself that change has happened and that you have found it hard to accept – until now!

The second thing is to understand just how important this change has been to you and what it means to your life. You have done this by circling all the emotions you feel about this change and that will show you just how important and significant this is to you. This is important, don't ignore it and pretend it doesn't matter – it does – it's your life and you matter!

In a cycle of continual change?

It helps to imagine change as a cycle of emotions and activities, so that you can see where you are in relation to this. Where are you in this cycle? Take a look and identify with where you feel you are right now.

Step 1

A change happens – a big or a small shock which could be any number of things.

Step 2

You experience a whole range of emotions and often shock and disbelief followed by either positive or negative emotions, depending on what it was.

Step 3

Generally a positive shock will mean that you will adjust and feel happy and positive quickly. Although apprehensive about the change or challenges to come, you may feel able to cope and look forward to the future and imagine ways in which you will learn to embrace this change. Getting married, having a baby, or a big promotion with a lot of responsibility would be good examples of this!

However, a negative shock might be harder to adjust to and feelings of confusion and being out of control may cause anxiety, anger, resentment, and then possibly sadness and real grief for something or someone who was always there and is now gone without you feeling prepared for that change.

Step 4

Feeling low and sad and out of control about the change in your life can leave you feeling stuck and overwhelmed and if it's been a particular change causing a big shock, then you may feel like this for a long time. But how long you continue to feel like this can be addressed and there will come a time when you want to move forward again.

Step 5

The important element to see in the cycle of change is that being stuck in a place of sadness and not being happy is not what your life is about. You have so much to give and live for, so finding your way out of this state will bring you good feelings and is the way forward. This is where you accept the change and decide the only way out is up again! Having acknowledged your feelings and then made a decision to feel good again it's time to focus on **HOW.**

Step 6

Moving on from the change into the future takes courage, but as soon as you begin to take action to change your life for the better you will begin to feel the positive effects. From this point on **the change is no longer controlling you and how you feel – YOU are back in control** and have decided to feel better, more positive and get back to living with a positive outlook and ready for the next challenge that life will throw at you. Now for **ACTION!**

Now you have acknowledged where you are on the cycle of change – **YOU CAN** do something about it now, and writing down your feelings (as you did previously from the above list) and then what you will start to do to change them is the step up again to positive feelings. Take a moment now to write down one action that will move you through this cycle and back in control again. Write down what that action is, what you need to do and when you are going to do it!

. . . .

. . . .

Brilliant! Now just go and do it – what have you got to lose?

What if...

Now is a good time to look at the *what if* question. It may be a good change that you wanted to happen, but it may also be a change that you didn't expect and you didn't see coming. Either way it's happened, so how do you deal with it positively and move forward again?

Ask yourself this question...

What if I stay as I am now and feel like this in one month's time? What will my life be like? Will my feelings affect my family, my health, my job, my friends?

Write your answer here:

. . . .
. . . .
. . . .
. . . .

What if I stay as I am now and feel like this in six months' time? What will my life be like? Will my feelings affect my family, my health, my job, my friends?

Write your answer here:

. . . .
. . . .
. . . .
. . . .

What if I accept responsibility for my own feelings and decide to do something positive to help myself move on. How will that help me and what effect will that have on my feelings in one month's time? What will my life be like? Will my feelings affect my family, my health, my job, my friends?

Write your answer here:

. . . .
. . . .
. . . .
. . . .

What if I accept responsibility for my own feelings and decide to do something positive to help myself move on. How will that help me and what effect will that have on my feelings in six months' time? What will my life be like? Will my feelings affect my family, my health, my job, my friends?

Write your answer here:

. . . .
. . . .
. . . .
. . . .

So now you know that ACTION is very important if you are going to make a positive change and move forward. Also, using this exercise whenever you face a change in your life will help you to make sense of what you feel, what you need and how you need to start taking positive action to move forward again instead of feeling stuck and overwhelmed.

How to embrace change

Would you feel more confident and positive about your life if you knew that no matter what happened to you, no matter what big or small changes lay around the corner ready to jump out and surprise you, you would be able to cope with it and be able to accept it no matter how hard, and move forward again? The answer lies in being aware of who you are and what is going on in your life. If you put your head in the sand when something is going wrong in your life or making you feel unhappy and uncomfortable, then that is the time to see it for what it is and not be afraid to be honest with yourself. At this crucial moment of awareness, it is time to look at what may be happening and what will happen if you don't address it now – you can feel in control of change if you stay prepared.

An example of confronting fear/change

A relationship that has gone off the boil and neither one of the couple is prepared to say what they really feel is the issue. Something has changed between them, but they put their heads in the sand and carry on regardless, for the sake of the children, for appearances sake or any other reason/excuse they give themselves! But both are unhappy and regularly get irritated and angry or resentful with each other. So whatever has happened between them has been ignored **(not acknowledged)** and therefore they can't even begin to be **honest about their feelings** about themselves or each other, and so they go on and on until they feel beyond irritated and resentful and become sad, desperate, unconnected and overwhelmed with the change that has happened to them. Now you can see that by moving through the cycle of change and being aware that it happens will give you confidence to embrace change without fear, because you know that you will find a way forward when you acknowledge honestly what you feel and need. The sooner a person becomes aware of a change happening, the better, but the key is to embrace this change and see it for what it is, if it is not clear what is happening, then expressing these thoughts or feelings is crucial in order to confront fear and change rather than ignore it until it becomes a serious issue.

Worry and fear stop action

We live in a worry culture, filled with fears, stress, tension, nervousness! If you often agitate over things that might go wrong, you may well be plagued by worry. Firstly you need to be aware that you do this in order to release the emotion of worry, notice the part of your body it most frequently inhabits. Don't judge yourself for worrying, but make friends with it, what does it feel like and sound like, so that you know when it's around. You might realize that being a person who worries so much may be an old habit connected to your past when it signified caring, soothing or sympathy for someone important in your life. By investing your energy in worrying for all the right reasons, it has now become a negative habit without you realizing.

So ask yourself, what purpose does this serve me now today? Is it really showing caring and comfort and sympathy to others or is it actually in control of me, and if I continue to worry, how is this going to affect my future?

Let go of the worry and anxiety for what it was and replace it with something positive you would like to feel. So for example when you know you would normally worry about something and get agitated, do something to make yourself laugh, this ignites happiness and positive feelings. People who worry tend to take themselves seriously and close down to fun and enjoyment which just makes anxiety levels even worse.

Practice laughter, go to a laughter workshop or watch a funny movie and have a good belly laugh!

By challenging yourself to move out of the worry state of mind, you will need to take action every time it happens and not sit and dwell on the worry. Get up physically, go for a walk, learn to dance, watch a movie, do something that will change your state of mind. Once you have done this, then come back to the thought that is worrying you and notice the difference, it will feel less significant because you decided to do something positive and take control of the feeling and replace it with a good feeling. This is something that gets easier with practice, the more you do it, the more you know you can lift your spirits with positive action!

Moving out of the comfort zone!

So let's say you acknowledge the change and how you feel about it and want to change this in a positive way. You even know what to do and there is nothing stopping you, then you hear that little voice of worry or the little voice of fear saying "You'd better not do that because it might not work" or "If you do that it might be worse" or even "Don't bother, you know it won't make any difference"! Any of that sound familiar? That's the little voice everyone has which in essence helps our self-preservation, but it also keeps us stuck in a comfort zone because nobody likes to fail. If you make a decision to change the way you feel and be positive, you have to challenge yourself not to give in to the doubting voice and take a small step that doesn't feel like a massive risk and then another and then another, before you know it, you've done it – you have moved out of that comfort zone!

Face it – life is a challenge

There are times in life when we feel like it is all an uphill struggle; people say things like "It never rains but it pours" and "Bad things all seem to happen at once"! However, we can progress through the challenges of life when we accept that life IS a struggle at times, it will not be all sweetness and light, things WILL go wrong at times and life is a constant flow of change. So before you get downhearted let's take this insight and turn it into something positive…

66 *Everything changes when* YOU *change.* 99

Anon

Learn to accept

Adapt to the challenges in life by reminding yourself of the positive things you do have in your life no matter what is happening to you. So when things are good look around and be grateful and when things get tough take a moment and write down a list of positives that will still exist in your life. It may feel strange to do this when you feel down because your brain will be in a negative state and won't be focusing on anything good, so this is where you need to help yourself by providing your brain with some reminders. Get out the photos of happy times you would like to remember, go through your qualifications or read your work experience profile and remind yourself how much you have done and achieved in life already. Go to a place that always makes you feel good because you had good times there or put that piece of music on that always brings a smile to your face. Remember your brain can be tricked into thinking it's happy and positive even when change is happening – you just have to give it the right information and it will remember happy times!

Take a note – keep a diary!

It makes a big difference if you write down and keep note of how you feel when life is challenging you. Make a point of making positive comments on your day or thoughts no matter how bad things get, as it's proven that writing down our thoughts, ideas and goals is 80% more effective than just thinking or talking about them. If you make a simple chart for each day of your diary by using a smiley face or a serious face or a sad face to indicate how you were feeling in the morning, afternoon and evening, this way if you don't have time to write anything down you can always do a quick scan of the day and see how you were feeling; ideally write a short note down next to the face so it explains the reason you were feeling up or down. This type of record of your feelings is a very helpful way to see if there are any patterns to your feelings over a period of time, usually a week or so is enough to look back over your feelings, and this will be an education for you to see how and why you are the way you are. The most important element of being able to embrace change is feeling that you can do something about change, that you feel empowered. If you know yourself well, how you feel and what makes you feel this way, then you are much closer to knowing what you can do about it to make it change for the better!

Connect thoughts and feelings

When you make a note in your diary, write down on a bit of paper or type a note on your personal computer about your thoughts that came up that day, it may help you to focus, relax and move forward. It doesn't matter if negative things have happened, the questions will help your mind assess the truth of what you are thinking and put it into perspective by being able to step back and look at it on paper. From this point you will find it easier to work out a solution.

Try this:

What have I done today for myself?

. . . .
. . . .

What have I done today for another person?

. . . .
. . . .

What have I learnt today about myself?

. . . .
. . . .

How can I be my best tomorrow and learn from today?

. . . .
. . . .

My own story

Some years ago I realized I was going through a very big change in my life and I thought that it would only be a positive experience if I could cope with this change and learn something about myself in the process. In order to do this I had to let go of the past and move on – 'easier said than done' I told myself!

Embracing any change is scary and that's a fact, even very nice exciting changes. I was not very confident in those days and I was worried that I would get it wrong again.

This is something I see all the time with my clients. We all go through difficult times and changes in our lives, it's how we deal with them that matters. What I managed to do and learnt how to help others do also, was to look beyond today, to focus on the good that is yet to come from the change.

In my case I needed to find somewhere to live, I had to find a job and had little money, my daughters needed their Mom to be home as I was a single parent after divorce and needed time to heal and recover my emotions. That's enough for anyone to sit and feel sorry for themselves and believe me I did for a while, but I looked at my girls and knew I wanted a better life for us all, to be a better Mom and so I called a Life Coach!

My life coach helped me to embrace change and feel my fears, just to go for it anyway! I had nothing to lose and only to gain. I began a 12-month plan to get fit and lose weight; find a place to live was first and then develop a career that I could balance around looking after my girls. I went back to school and then to university and as you know, trained in life coaching because it helped me so much, I wanted to give something back.

No matter what the change you are going through, grab it by the horns and take responsibility for what you want the outcome to be. You can do something about it, it is possible. I know, I've been there, and turned my life around!

Summary

- One thing you can be sure of, life will keep presenting you with change, but it's how you deal with it that will determine your success.

- If you fear change, then using a coach to help you understand what is behind that fear will give you clarity and choice of how to get past those fears.

- Writing down times of change in your life will help you to identify the highs and lows and understand how you handle change.

- If change is something we can't stop, then learning to accept this will help us to maintain and re-balance life when we need to.

- The more important someone or something is to us, the harder it is when things change and we hang on and refuse to change. This only holds us back.

- It helps to image change as a cycle of emotions, moving through stages and coming out the other side – ready for the next change!

- Being stuck in a negative cycle of sadness and unhappiness because of change we didn't want or ask for, can feel like being trapped or stuck; accepting all the emotions of change will help us move on.

- Asking the 'what if' questions helps to understand and become aware of our thoughts and behavior which might be resisting change.

- Worry and fear develop into stress, tension and frustration. Don't invest your energy into worry and fear, turn it into positive action.

- Keeping a diary of your goals and feelings can be a more effective way to express yourself than just talking about them; it helps you to move forward.

Finding your Passion

" *Just because they're your beliefs, don't be fooled into thinking that they always act in your best interests.* **"**

Anon

Chapter 3
Finding your Passion

Life Coaching is not about changing yourself, but rather about becoming yourself, helping you to develop your passion and motivation for the life you want to live!

The more you know about yourself, what you love, what you dislike, what makes you excited, what fills you with a passion for life and what makes you motivated, then the easier it is for you to set goals and achieve what you need in order to be happy.

Feeling motivated to live a life full of passion and happiness is possible when you are honest with who you are and what you really want! But here's the thing, most of us think we know who we are and what we want out of life, wake up and go to bed doing the same things every day and yet as the years go by something seems to change. Our passion for the life we would love to have has declined, we accept our lot, we move into a comfortable place (the comfort zone) and settle back, no longer wanting to take the risk to be who we really are. But why does this happen?

The word NO stops passion!

Children are enthusiastic and motivated to learn, to survive and grow, it is a basic instinct. However, as we grow up and begin to understand the world around us, our parents, teachers and peers begin to influence our understanding of who we are, what we can or cannot do and what will happen if we do our own thing and not what they consider to be the right thing! For very good reasons a parent will say no as a child goes to run across a busy street or is in danger.

However, the natural enthusiasm and motivation we are all born with is slowly influenced by the experiences we have and the most powerful experience we feel is love. So to be loved or liked and wanted, we learn to curb who we are and what we want in order to maintain this emotion or connection. As this emotion is also a basic instinct of survival, it's there inside us for a reason, to keep us together as human beings and maintain the human race. The problem comes when we give up who we are in order to achieve and maintain this love connection; we lose sight of what we may have originally wanted because it became more important to us to feel loved.

Do you know who you are?

So here's the question, if you know who you are, you will know what you value! Do you know what you value and what is most important to you?

We all value things, but what exactly are your life values, the things in life that are very important to you and give you a happy feeling when these values and needs are being met?

The challenge in life is to understand what you value first, this is who YOU are, and then live a life which reflects these values honestly in what you hold most important. This is not easy as some people may feel this is being selfish, however, following what other people value is not being true to yourself.

What do you value the most?

When you know what your personal values are, you will be on track with directing your life forward. Take a moment to write down what you value. I've included some examples and you can circle the ones you think apply to you and add more of your own...

Love	Compassion	Honesty	Respect
Freedom	Passion	Intimacy	Happiness
Fun	Security	Health	Creativity
Contributing	Learning	Adventure	Achievement
Personal Growth	Caring	Excitement	Power
Success	Independence	Sharing	Winning

Now if you think about what you have chosen and how important these values are to you, then you will be able to imagine how living a life that enables you to express and experience these values would make you incredibly happy and passionate about your life.

What's missing for you?

When you have identified the most important values in your life, you can look at whether these values are being met, because if not, you now have a choice to do something about it. For example, if creativity is something you value and therefore need in your life, allowing yourself to build into your life the things you truly value will give you back your passion and this in turn will help you feel fulfilled, happy, secure, expressed, increase your energy levels instead of feeling stuck and unfulfilled. Its worth pointing out here that we sometimes fall into the trap of thinking it's too late to change things or that we need something or someone else to change before we can have what we need. Is this really true – asking yourself honestly, have you used this as an excuse not to do what YOU need to do in order to be happy? Don't let those negative thoughts, regrets or limiting beliefs creep in and stop you from helping yourself to live a happy life.

Lighting the torch of passion!

Here is where the truth comes in; how are you going to live a life filled with passion and motivation if you ignore what you value most? The key is to find ways to live out the things you value the most and not deny they exist. Write down below how you can meet your values in your life, take the words you circled above and expand on them to give yourself an explanation of what you need in order to experience these values in your life, for example…

Love . . . . to love and be loved.

Compassion . . . . . to express my compassion towards others.

Creativity . . . . to be creative.

Adventure. . . . . . . to experience adventure.

Fun. . . . . to have fun in my life.

Respect. . . . . to respect myself and expect respect in return.

Health. . . . . to take responsibility for my health and to care for my body.

To help you understand what a 'value' is, try thinking of something you may value already, for example being 'creative'. Now imagine not being able to be creative ever again in your life, not being able to appreciate creativity in yourself, in others, in what you see and feel; imagine it just does not exist! If you feel like it would be an empty life, that something very important is missing, then this is something you value and simply MUST have in your life in order to feel complete!

?..

?..

?..

?..

?..

?..

?..

?..

?..

?..

?..

?..

?..

?..

?..

?..

?..

?..

You can make your own list – all you have to do to increase your passion is be TRUE to who you are.

> **" *If you have the courage to begin – you have the courage to succeed.* "**

Anon

Motivated by honesty

Once you're clear about your values and you feel the passion for the life you want, you can begin to set your goals, and your goals are simply to improve these areas of your life. The motivation to change your life for the better comes from the truth of who you really are and what you really want. In the chapter about goals you can take this truth and look at all the areas of your life and begin to set out your personal goals.

Being authentic

Can you remember a time when you made a decision in your life and it just felt right? If you can, then chances are you will understand that you were being real and authentic. This takes courage and comes from the heart; it feels instinctive and sometimes even spiritual. By learning to be authentic about who you are and how you may feel afraid to be yourself, you can release the truth of what you truly want and then you'll be able to make decisions straight from the heart with passion and honesty.

This is not an easy thing to do, we set up all sorts of barriers and stay in our comfort zones, limiting beliefs and excuses to avoid facing these truths; but the reality is, the most successful people in life are the ones who face their fears and act from a place of authenticity, and this is where they feel a sense of freedom and release for who they are.

When I say successful I am not referring to money and financial success, I am talking about happiness and what that means to an individual; whether that be being a great mother, teacher, friend, leader, partner – it's being yourself and the best of yourself comes from being real.

What blocks motivation?

FEAR...............blocks motivation. Be really honest with yourself here. What are you really afraid of? Who are you pretending to be? If you have identified who you really are and how you would like your life to be, then there must be a reason why you have not changed this before. Right? What is this reason?

You might even be reading this book and thinking, yes this is all very interesting but it doesn't apply to me, I'm not afraid of anything, I have no fears really. However, if you have things that you do wish were different and you could do something about it and have not yet – then you must have a reason and therefore fears creep in and stop us from taking action to change things.

To help you – here is an example of one person's life when they answered this question. To give you some background, this person had come through a very painful and difficult divorce over a period of years and had lost their confidence, had low self esteem and had a negative belief about themselves not being worthy to be as happy as others.

They asked these questions and gave themselves these answers:

Q. Who would I like to be?

A. Attractive, happy, interesting and loved.

Q. Who am I being/pretending to be?

A. Unattractive, unhappy, feeling stupid and unlovable.

Q. How do I benefit from thinking like this?

A. I don't have to take responsibility to change myself and fail; I don't have to risk being hurt again.

Q. What is the price I'm paying?

A. I don't like myself or the way I look, my health suffers, my children have a parent with no confidence, I am alone, I am unhappy and I feel guilty for not being a better person – it's affecting everything.

So can you see what this person was doing? Their self belief was very negative and this couldn't be changed until they looked at the truth of what they were doing to themselves – they were being controlled by **FEAR** – fear that they were not good enough!

Once this person was honest about who they really were – attractive, happy, interesting and lovable, it was then up to them to begin acting like that and being true to themselves. They didn't have to change anything actually, they just needed to be authentic about who they really were and wanted to be!

This person was me back in the days before I became a coach and it took courage to face the way I was behaving and to be honest with myself, but it was the best thing I have ever done and I have never looked back. I use this format of questions any time I feel a bit stuck or unsure of my feelings and it works. There is nothing better to give a negative state of mind a good shake up and face the truth, so I can fix it for myself.

Are you feeling brave?

Go on then, try this for yourself! Write down honestly the answers to these questions and learn to take responsibility for what you think of yourself, so that you can make better decisions.

Who would I like to be?

. . . .
. . . .

Who am I being or pretending to be?

. . . .
. . . .

How do I benefit from thinking like this?

. . . .
. . . .

What is the price I have to pay?

. . . .

. . . .

Well done! That took courage, but you did it!

Create your dream board

Have some fun here and use your imagination to create a life that you would like to experience. This is where you can go wild and add things to your dream board that will inspire you and develop your motivation. Take a big piece of paper or a writing board and create a collage of images based on what you would like to experience. You could use images cut out of magazines, words, inspirational quotations, book titles, photos of people you admire or who inspire you, places you want to visit, things you want to do, even down to the food you would like to eat! Remember to keep in mind the things that you value in life and whatever images/dream you come up with. Ask yourself: Is this really me? Do I really want this? Will it fulfil my values?

When you've finished doing your board, it should look bright and full of inspiration for you. Pin it up somewhere you can see it and use it to motivate you into action and look at it daily, think about what it means to you and why it's important for you. Add things to it when you think of something new, fun or exciting that inspires you. I have one in my office and over the years I have added little notes and images of things I would like to achieve or experience. It's amazing to look at it now and see that many of these things have been realized. There is no doubt that if you make your goals very vivid and focus on them, it will be a powerful way to help you achieve them, as your brain allows you to believe over time by looking at these images of what makes you happy, that this is who you are, what you want and will create in your life.

" Focus on where you want to go – not on what you fear. "

Anon

Patience and little steps

It is important to point out that it is human nature to want everything that makes us happy right now! However, look upon your dream board as a way to inspire you with your goals and then develop an action plan and take small steps forward, one thing at a time. *(This is covered in Chapter 4: Setting Personal Goals.)*

Building confidence fuels passion

A lot of confidence comes from our self-image, because how we think and feel about our own image affects our confidence. Today's society is extremely image conscious and it can often feel like a constant pressure from visual advertising on how we should appear and what success is meant to look like. This is one way we are reminded on a daily basis that we are not measuring up to the norm, but let's be realistic here, the norm is generated from big business marketing campaigns to get us buying as much as possible. So it's no wonder many of us are constantly unhappy with our self-image because we are trying to achieve the impossible, therefore we are always dissatisfied with what we look like. The fact is that these perfect images of success are set unrealistically high for a reason – to keep us in a state of dissatisfaction with ourselves; we will never be able to attain them and therefore feel cheated and disheartened that whatever we achieve it never feels like enough, so we keep trying to achieve more and more in the hope that one day we will reflect what the advertisements tell us happiness is!

So that's my little rant and rave over, mainly because as a parent it is vital that we look after our inner confidence and not let the economic, social and public pressure dictate who we really are inside. Don't get me wrong though, improving your image and appearance and developing a strong and confident attitude and body posture, the way you behave and the way you speak to others, can make you look and feel more confident.

So let's start…

Be passionate about who you are

Confidence and a positive self image comes from feeling good about yourself and being comfortable with exactly who you are, so as much as you can, RESIST being pulled into the media models of image and success. Find a person who you identify with and make it someone that you admire for being truly themselves. Look at how they express themselves and become more of who they are, rather than less.

Who do you admire?

Make a list of people you think are confident and express this, and then start to explore by writing down the things about yourself that you admire and like. For example you may be a great person to have as a friend, have artistic talents, enjoy singing, be good at your job, enjoy cooking, have nice hair, a lovely smile, whatever it is. Think about how this is a positive element of who you are, allow to like yourself and take credit for it.

Stop comparing

Now we all have people we admire and I must admit that some people are just beautiful and clever and so on, however, it's a good idea to stop comparing yourself with others because whilst you are doing that you are not looking at your true self and admiring and developing the great qualities you have. Begin by admitting to yourself that there will always be someone lovelier, cleverer, and more interesting, more exciting etc. and that it is normal to want to be your best. The next step is to look at yourself as an *original* – a unique person in your own right. Take a few minutes now to think about whether you compare yourself to others and how this makes you feel; commit to **stop** doing this and realize that you are a very special person and there is only **ONE** of you in the whole world – you are totally unique – how amazing and priceless is that!

Act with confidence

There will always be times when we feel a bit negative about ourselves, this is natural. All sorts of things can influence our emotions and that's what makes us different and interesting. Being aware of how we feel is important, and taking some time to help ourselves is about taking responsibility for that. The next time you feel negative about things, remember that it is *a thought, a feeling* and write that feeling down on a big enough piece of paper to stand on with both feet; then I want you to write down the feeling you do want to have on another sheet of paper. Place them both on the floor and stand on the negative one that you are experiencing at that moment. Stand on it for a few moments and allow yourself to think about why, what and how it is that you feel, take it all in and then when you are ready move off the paper onto the positive one, read it and think about it in your mind, imagine what that feeling feels like; perhaps you have gone from feeling angry and sad to happy and uplifted, so think about the positive feelings and imagine yourself experiencing them. Notice how you feel physically and lift your head up as you step off the paper. Now finally, take the sheet of paper with the negative feelings and rip it up into small pieces and bin it!

Wow! That feels good and every time you need a boost do this exercise and train your brain that it has a choice to think negatively or positively! If necessary get a big enough bin especially for the job!

Pressing the self-destruct button?

You know 90% of what we worry about **never** actually happens, and yet while we sit and think and worry about things we don't realize that our negativity is producing other negative experiences, and sometimes what we worry about can actually happen because we are so focused on this we lose sight of all the positive things. I can give you a funny example of this; I remember baking a cake for my daughter's 5th birthday and it was a new recipe, so I wasn't sure how it was going to turn out; I was worried that it wouldn't rise in the oven and then it would be a disaster for the birthday party with no cake! As a result I checked on the oven at least three times, opening the door each time to see that it was baking properly – you know what happened! Of course it flopped in the oven because the cold air went in every time I opened the door! So you see, I created the one thing I was worrying about! My lack of confidence and fear actually created the very thing I did not want.

I know this is a trivial example, but I have done this in so many other ways in my life, that I am now very aware when I start to worry about things that I have to be careful that I am not being self-destructive!

Take a moment now to think about whether you do this and commit to change this in yourself by **asking a different question** about your concerns or worries.

Questions you might like to ask yourself:

Q. If I worry about this, is it going to make any difference at all?

Q. Is there any action I can take that will make a positive difference?

Q. Can I decide to stop worrying about this? Yes or No.

Q. What is the benefit I receive from worry?

Q. If I worry about this – is it allowing me to avoid something else?

Be a completer

One of the fastest ways to give yourself confidence and a real boost to your self esteem is to complete what you started. Now that might sound obvious, but we all suffer from this and start off with the best intentions – such as New Year resolutions – with ideas and interests that feel exciting at the time, but then many don't get past the thinking about it part. Then there are all the half completed jobs that keep niggling in the back of your mind and the putting off becomes days, then weeks, then a month goes by and for some things, even years!

Make a list of all the things you wanted to do and started but have not finished – it could be sorting out a room at home, tidying your office, clearing the garage, decorating the house, writing that book or joining that club, whatever it was, decide if you still want or need to do it and why. If the reason is a good one, then make it a priority and take action on it today. Allow yourself the pleasure and happiness of feeling really good that you finished something you said you were going to do and YOU DID!

Say what you mean!

Practice saying what you mean – not what you think people want to hear. Be yourself and listen to your internal voice that tells you what you would like to say. There are always times when it is wise to say nothing and to wait for a better moment, but on the whole, if you practice being clear about what you really want to say it can save a whole lot of worry and misunderstanding. Easy to say I know, but start to practice it with someone you would really like to be straight with, perhaps you know a person who is always judgemental of others or makes negative comments. Why not start with this person and commit to saying something positive or what you really mean the next time you see them.

For example, a relative or person makes an unnecessary comment; you could go along with it and join in, or imagine how liberating it would feel to say "Well actually I don't agree, I think ....". By doing this you are taking control of your life and this will give you confidence in other things. Often the people we find it the hardest to say what we mean to are those closest to us.

Write down a list of those people with whom you find it hard to say what you mean and next to the name write down what you would like to say to them.

Now take the easiest one on your list and commit to make a small step in the right direction by saying exactly what you mean the next time you see them. It doesn't have to be a big thing, but it does need to be what you would like to say and not what you think they want to hear! Go on, go for it – you know you want to!

Positive talk and feedback

I really like it when people are straightforward and say what they mean, even though I know it is sometimes hard to hear, especially if I'm asking a question and their answer throws me.

Of course there is a way of saying what you mean and this comes with confidence. I take the view that, if it is going to help someone to talk straight with them, then this is the best thing to do, even if it feels hard to do. Talk straight with yourself first and act with positivity.

Who needs to know?

Often giving feedback to others reflects our own fears or misunderstanding of another person. To be sure that the feedback we give or the need we have to tell another person how we feel is justified, try writing a letter to yourself first putting in all the things you want to say and why you need to say it, how you feel and how you feel it will help them. Read the letter through a couple of times and if possible with a day or two between writing it and reading it again. Now ask yourself who is going to benefit from the letter? Does the letter (or feedback) really need to be given or has writing it down had a positive effect and you have learnt something about yourself by doing it?

In my experience, there is no such thing as constructive criticism, it is criticism and words do stick in people's hearts and minds. Ask yourself – do your words build this person or do they knock them down? Then you will know what to do.

Living with passion

When you have the courage to say what you need and want in life, both to yourself and others, it allows you to discover and live your passion.

This passion could be anything from making music to saving lives, but it's a truth that you live out in your attitude to yourself. My clients discover their passion when we go through their coaching programme and look at what their goals are. They often find that their passion has been drowned out over many years with negative beliefs or experiences and this is what we address in the coaching in order to free the passion that has always been there, but they have blocked out.

I discovered my passion when I discovered who I was first. I then gave myself permission to live out and express who I was and what I valued in my life, such as being healthy, empowering others, dancing, being a business woman and a mother, the list is endless. In essence it all comes down to being honest with what you need and want in your life – focus on yourself and get that right first.

I help my clients to understand that once you are honest with yourself and start to live out what you want, then the passion begins to flow and it becomes like a snowball effect, whereby the more you practice the things that make you happy and give you a sense of self, the happier you become and the passion grows and grows. It's like a magnet that attracts the right things, the right people, and so many opportunities to you it can sometimes feel a bit freaky. Some people believe that this passion is a positive universal energy that generates from being connected to your true self and in turn it allows you to feel connected to everything important to you, which is so exciting and fills your heart with passion and energy for more.

Summary

- Looking inside yourself to what you really love or dream and being honest with who you are will develop your passion.

- Getting stuck in the 'comfort zone' will put out the light of passion and motivation.

- We are all born with natural enthusiasm and passion, motivation to be our best. Don't give up who you really are and always hold onto your dreams.

- If you know who you are, you will know what you value; if you know what you value, and then develop a life that fulfils those values, you will be living with passion.

- If you have lost sight of what you would like or dream of having, create a dream board – collecting images, ideas and quotes in one place to inspire you.

- Self-image affects confidence, so take pride in this to develop a strong and confident attitude.

- Feel comfortable about who you are and resist the pull of media models and images of success; be passionate about who you are – you are unique!

- Connect with someone you admire and look at the qualities this person has; write down how you could develop these positive elements inside yourself.

- 90% of what we worry about never actually happens and negativity produces self-destructive behavior.

- Finish things off, it's a good feeling when you complete something you started.

- Practice saying what you mean and not what you think people want you to say.

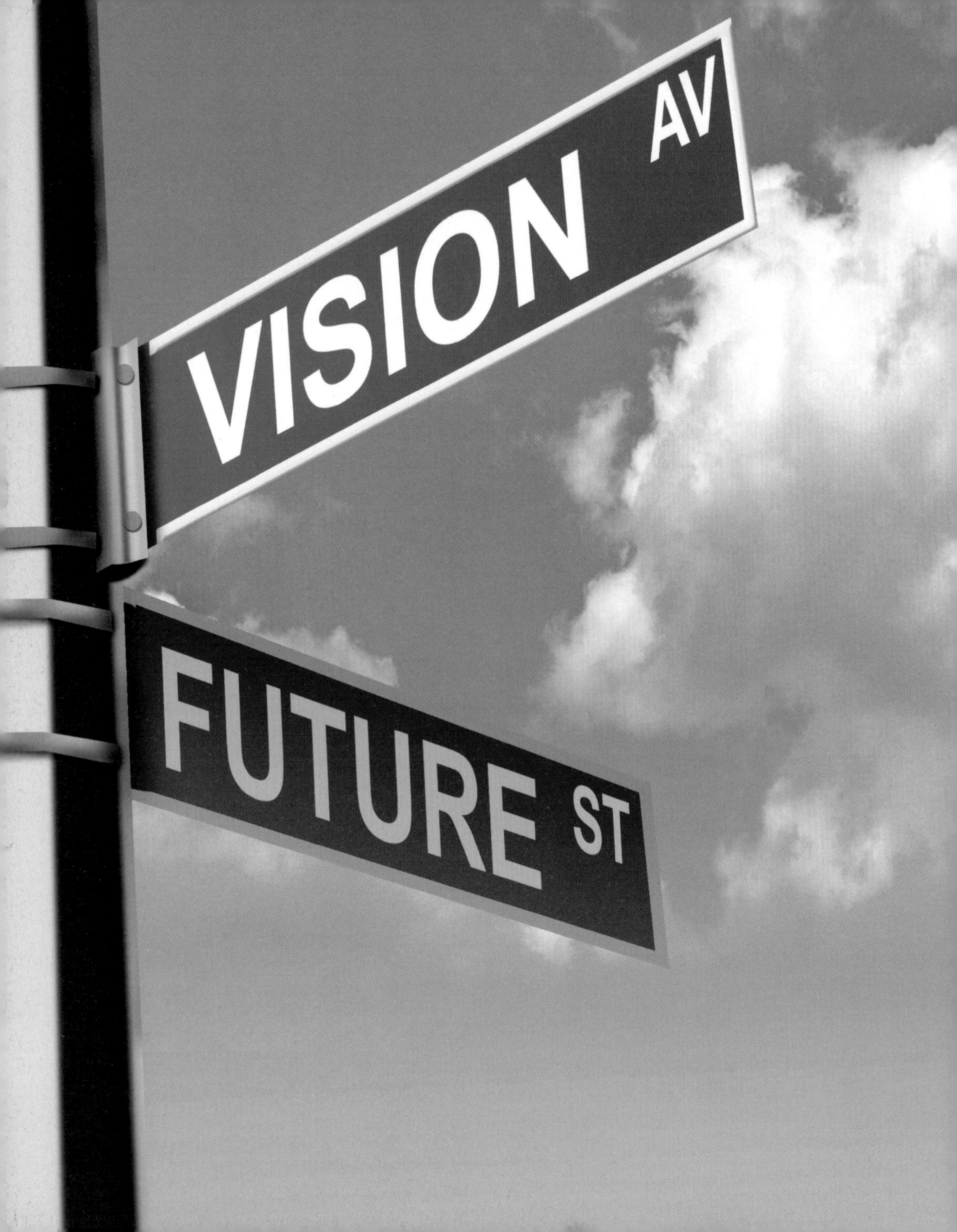
VISION AV
FUTURE ST

Setting Personal Goals

" Life changes the moment you make a decision to commit to developing yourself – to know oneself is to think for oneself! "

Anon

Chapter 4
Setting Personal Goals

Knowing exactly what you really want is a big question, but it's all important if you are going to create a happy and fulfilling life; but knowing why you want those things in your life is the key to moving forward and having the life you want. So in order to understand what motivates you it is essential that you know what you value and what is important to you, this is what makes you as a person and directs you to the things in life you want to feel and experience. *(See Chapter 3: Finding your passion.)*

A great place to start is by asking yourself some honest questions about how happy you are with all the different areas of your life. Often it is a lack of confidence that stops people feeling clear about what they want and setting their goals. Are you as confident as you would like to be? To feel confident in yourself you will need to feel confident that it is possible to succeed in what you really want and to believe that your ambitions, needs, and deepest desires really do matter!

So by working on this area of your life and being really honest with yourself about your life right now, it will help you to set goals to make positive changes and help you to see clearly what you really want; this will motivate you forward, then moving one step at a time to gain confidence from addressing the things you want to change or improve in your life.

Develop your strengths

Take a pen and write your name vertically down the page here and for each letter I want you to write something positive about yourself.

So for example my name is Simone and here are words I, or others, have said about me which are positive.

(Space here for your name)

S = sensitive
I = interesting
M = motivating
O = optimistic
N = natural
E = enthusiastic

Just have a play with the words and remember they can be words to describe who you are or what you do, or even how you would like to be, as long as they are positive!

Now imagine having a go at listing your strengths and write down what makes you special and wonderful. Would you find this easy to do?

How about writing down a list of your weaknesses? Many people find it easier to list these than the positives. We are generally pretty hard on ourselves, and you may be hiding behind the fact that you are actually afraid of being positive and truly expressing your strengths. So what are your strengths exactly?

Create affirmations

Support what you feel about yourself with an affirmation. Give yourself some positive statements about yourself which are all in the present tense. For example, how about one of these or a mix of them; whatever you believe about yourself, even if you are not convinced – try it now!

I am attractive and intelligent.
I am good at my job.
I am a great person.
I am special and interesting.

I am ....

....

....

....

Whatever you decide, write down your affirmation here in the space provided and read it over and over and then say it to yourself each morning. Whatever you focus your attention on is what the brain is responding to. Remember it is easy to fill your brain with worries and negative thoughts, so block them out and create a new positive thought process that is empowering for you!

Do you know what your goals are?

See the list on pages 74–75 of the most common life areas that people feel are important and of value to them, although they may not be exactly the same for everyone, it's a good place to start. Take a look at each area and think about how you feel about each one. This is just for you to see, so go on be really honest about it and don't miss anything out.

Write out the life areas below and score them from 1 to 10 for how happy and content you are with each one. 1 being a low score because you are very unhappy about it, 9 or 10 because it's just perfect and maybe a 5 or 6 for an area that needs improvement. Once you have written down the score for each, take a look at how the scores impact on each other. For example, money is often related to work and home, whereas a low score on partner might have an impact on health and well-being, and particularly your emotional well-being!

Now look at your scores

Great, so now you have given them all a score and made some connections to areas that influence each other, you will be able to see both negative and positive connections. What you may find interesting is that the area that is the highest score is the one area that you have no problem putting a lot of time, effort and energy into. You enjoy working on this part of your life because you value it very highly and you gain happiness and pleasure from making an effort in this area.

However, the scores that are lower may be the ones you have been avoiding because they feel painful or you find them difficult to address. The important thing to remember here is about working to achieve balance in all these areas of your life. As you will see, when one area is out of balance it will have a knock-on effect on the other areas of your life. It is also important to point out that as we all strive to achieve a good balance in all these areas, sometimes things come along in life that we did not expect and throw great plans out of the window. However, you now know that you can do this exercise any time you feel things are out of balance and see exactly where the challenges are for you and how they are making you feel, so that you can address the balance and do something about it.

Score a goal!

The scores that are low become your goals. To improve those areas in your life, you can begin to be specific now and look at exactly what you would need to do to improve the scores by just one mark to start with!

First let's imagine that you don't do anything about these scores at all except just look at them and then close the book and move on. I want you to imagine now what your life will look like in 12 months' time and having done nothing about any of the scores to improve them I want you to score them again; what will have happened if you just left everything as it is? And if that begins to look negative, I then want you to move forward in time another two years and imagine where you live, your work, family, health, relationship and having done nothing about those low scores now for three years, what does you life look like?

" *Always look at how far you have come – not how far you have to go.* "

Anon

Here are the 8 life areas:

Health and well-being

This is about all the areas of your health and well-being, so how do you feel about your emotional, mental, physical and spiritual sense of well-being? How much positive energy do you feel?

Score . . . .

Work and Career

How is your work and do you have the career you want or are you working towards this area of your life? Are there any difficulties here?

Score . . . .

Money

This one is interesting – we often feel like we don't have enough, but be honest and ask yourself is this really the case? What do you really need to be happy?

Score . . . .

Family and Friends

How are your relationships here, do you have enough time for your family, parents, children? Is it quality time? Are there difficulties?

Score . . . .

Partner

Whether or not you have a partner or someone special to share your life with, the important thing is how you feel about it, honestly!

Score . . . .

Personal Development

Are you learning new things about yourself and others and developing as a human being? An example might be new motherhood, doing a training course, studying for a job, traveling or contributing to others.

Score . . . .

Fun and Leisure

Ah yes, do you get time for this? Do you make time for it? Do you do too much of it and not enough of other things that you know are important to you? This area is just as important as anything else.

Score . . . .

Environment or Home

Where you live, your neighborhood, the home you live in and the people you live with or near to, all have an impact on how you feel.

Score . . . .

Taking action now

If you want to improve those scores then now you will begin to understand the force of what motivates you. Perhaps it is to change something to move away from it or to move towards something better; whichever it is, you will now begin to see how to find your motivation easily if you are honest enough with who you are and what will happen if you don't take responsibility yourself for what you want.

Taking action is absolutely crucial to moving forward and when you move forward you will automatically feel your confidence growing. As you become more and more true to yourself, you will be able to feel your inner confidence and inner strength develop. Many people talk a lot about what they will do, they even feel motivated and passionate about changing things, however, it is only when action is actually taken that there is a physical, mental and emotional shift and a new energy released, this is the energy that makes you feel happy and confident.

Making a commitment!

Choose the area in your life that you feel is **the most important right now** and which you know will have the biggest impact on your life if you take steps to improve it. Choose one of these and write down your goal next to it:

Health and Well-being . . . .

Work and Career . . . .

Money . . . .

Partner . . . .

Personal Development . . . .

Fun and Leisure. . . . .

Environment/Home. . . . .

My goal is:

. . . .
. . . .

I am going to take the following action now to move one step closer to my
goal and to become more true to myself:

. . . .
. . . .

I am going to take this action (when exactly?):

. . . .
. . . .

I am committed to this first step, the only thing holding me back is:

. . . .
. . . .

I am going to overcome this by taking action on:

. . . .
. . . .

Now I am 100% committed to my goal and it starts NOW!

CONGRATULATIONS!

Gemma's story

Living abroad in another country and traveling to experience different cultures was Gemma's dream. She had decided to have some life coaching though to get past her fears and plan what she needed to do. She knew it was going to change her life and she was very apprehensive.

Gemma was stuck in a bad job, had no savings and was scared that she would never get to travel and live her dream. It all seemed rather impossible and she was full of stories when we met about things happening to girls traveling alone and ultimately she was scared.

We set to work planning her dream goals with time scales and a vision of her ideal life abroad and then with this very clear picture we began to work backwards planning each step of her journey to the present moment in time.

We looked at the practical elements, such as how much money she would need, how could she earn this money in order to save enough for her trip, what changes she needed to make in her current lifestyle to help her focus and achieve her dream.

We planned where she would live abroad and the work she could do there, she researched and organized as the time went by and then the day came one year later, she had saved enough money, had sacrificed not having everything she wanted that year and stayed focused on her goal. Off she went traveling with a place arranged for her to live, friends she could meet up with traveling and even a job in her dream location.

From a complete pipe dream to reality, Gemma set off on her travels with such confidence and was so proud of herself and embraced her life abroad with no fear – only excitement. Gemma had overcome her fears because she focused on what she really wanted and then took responsibility to make it happen. It took planning and focus, but she did what she thought was always going to be impossible and loves it.

Summary

- Being goal focused ensures that you are a forward looking and positive person; this will increase your chances of success in life.

- Looking at all the areas of your life and scoring them will highlight what is working and what is not; with this greater awareness you can begin to set goals to improve them.

- Moving one step at a time towards your goals will ensure you don't worry about failing. Move at the pace that you feel comfortable with.

- Giving yourself positive affirmations about your strengths will encourage motivation.

- When you see an area of your life working well, know that this is where you are putting in particular energy and effort. The opposite is true of areas in your life that are not working well.

- Looking at your life 12 months from now will help you to become aware of the impact that not working on your goals will have on your life.

- Take action to move forward with your goals and dreams. You must 'do' and get into the habit of taking action on a daily basis.

- Practice being solution focused on anything that feels like a problem or challenge, taking a 'can do it' approach will keep you positive.

- People who write goals down are 80% more likely to achieve them than those that don't.

- If you don't take action to achieve the results you want in your life, then who will do it for you? Taking 100% responsibility for your life is the first goal to master.

Well-being & Life Balance

*" **Don't waste ill health,**
use it to heal your life! "*

Richard Wilkins

Chapter 5
Well-being & Life Balance

Well-being means our whole life where we are achieving a sense of balance in our health and the food we eat, our working lives and relationships, our fun, adventures and leisure time as well as our personal sense of achievement or sense of fulfillment.

It makes sense that having good health and a real sense of well-being will give us a better chance of achieving the life we want. No amount of money or wonderful material assets we gather in our lives will be worth anything to us if we don't have a mind and body to enjoy it all.

Well-being and lasting change

The words *well-being* are used all the time to describe and sell everything from the latest diets to face creams, food for our children, and endless marketing campaigns use it on television and the Internet in order to get us interested in their products. However, don't be put off by hearing these words all the time; to bring about lasting changes we need to decide which areas of our lives are going well and which ones need improving. Staying motivated and taking small steps with clear goals is a lot easier than taking huge leaps into the unknown. *(See Chapter 3: Finding your Passion and Chapter 4: Setting Personal Goals.)*

So how is your well-being today?

How do you feel now, do you have a sense of well-being? Is your life in balance? Using the selection of words others have used before to describe well-being, take a moment to circle the words below that you would use for yourself and add any others that you consider important!

Calm	Content	Fulfilled	Peaceful
Happy	Healthy	Fit	Energized
Spiritual	Sense of purpose	Control	Connected
Joyful	Grateful	Respected	Confident

Do you feel this in your life? Do you have that sense of life balance and well-being?

If you do then that's a great place to be and you can look at how to maintain that with your goals. If you don't have that feeling, then circle the ones you would like to feel and this can help you with your goal setting!

Visualize health and well-being

Learn how to improve your health and well-being and you will have a much better chance of creating the life you want. Take a moment to try this visualization technique and imagine your **body is a car...!**

Imagine you were going on a round the world trip and needed to buy a car for the journey. Would you buy a car that had no air in the tires or water and oil in the engine? Or a car that had not been serviced and was struggling to start when you put the key in? Would this car fill you with excitement and security about your long journey ahead? OK, so joking apart, imagine your body is the car, you expect it to get you through the journey of your life without letting you down, but do you look after it and make sure it is fit for the job? Most of us take our bodies for granted until something goes wrong. So it makes sense to look after our bodies and keep them healthy, which in turn will give us confidence to face life's ups and downs.

Make a commitment today to give your body what it needs. Start by giving yourself a reality check and this will also provide you with more motivation!

Ask yourself these questions and write down the answers

How do I rate my sense of well-being today out of 1-10? Score . . . .

Give yourself an overall score and then ask yourself the questions below.

1. How long can my body cope with this?

. . . .
. . . .

2. What can I do to help myself?

. . . .
. . . .

3. What will happen if I don't bother?

. . . .
. . . .

4. When can I begin to do this?

. . . .
. . . .

Healthy pressure or unhealthy stress?

Do you understand the difference between pressure and stress? We live in a culture that is constantly focusing on stress, however it's important to remember that not all stress is bad! For example, sitting an exam, competing in a race or competition, going for a job interview or even getting married all create a certain level of pressure or stress. However, we know through research that this can be a positive pressure and working under a certain amount of pressure is exciting and motivating, some people actually thrive on high levels of pressure. The problem comes when unhealthy amounts of pressure turn into feelings of stress, which if not dealt with will persist and take its toll on our health and overall well-being – then we begin to feel beaten up by the stress.

Managing stress

Learning how to manage the stresses you experience in life ensures you maintain your health and well-being, as stress (when it is stored up and not dealt with) will start to impact on your health. It's not always easy to recognize in yourself when you are suffering from too much pressure and you are becoming stressed. The first step to help yourself is to take a coaching perspective on what good health and well-being means to you, and from this point you will begin to recognize the areas in your life that cause you to feel stressed and how the negative effects of stress are affecting you and your life. You are now able to set clear goals to ensure you beat stress before it beats you!

Know your body – your stress triggers

Knowing your body and how you behave under pressure is the first important step in taking control of negative stress. Here is a list of some of the behaviors that may be triggered in you when you start to show signs of feeling stressed. It's important to remember that everyone is different and what would make some people feel under pressure and stressful can be exciting for others. Think about a time when you felt under a lot of pressure in your life – it could be at work, school, home, family, relationships – and what were your stress triggers.

> ❝ *The human body is the best picture of the human soul.* ❞

Ludwig Wittgenstein

- Low on energy and always tired.

- Headaches and muscle tension.

- Not sleeping well and restless at night.

- Rushing all the time everywhere.

- Overeating or eating food you don't usually eat.

- Over drinking or having drinks you usually don't have.

- Feeling moody and snappy.

- Taking more exercise or ceasing to exercise.

- Feeling anxious and jumpy.

- Feeling overwhelmed and unfulfilled.

- Feeling emotional and tearful.

- Feeling forgetful and confused.

Can you relate to any of these feelings, behaviors and symptoms?

Write down here the things you recognize in yourself when you begin to feel stressed so you can use it as a way of reminding yourself to take notice and do something positive to help yourself feel better:

. . . .
. . . .
. . . .
. . . .
. . . .
. . . .
. . . .
. . . .
. . . .

What I can do to take the pressure off

Write down here the things you have done in the past that have worked to help you feel more relaxed and in control, ask yourself when you last did this for yourself and how would it benefit you today to do this when you feel your stress triggers:

. . . .
. . . .
. . . .
. . . .
. . . .
. . . .

Positive psychology

Positive psychology provides a way forward in understanding who you are and how you feel about your life. Take a look at the following areas to see how your feelings of mental well-being associated with good work-life balance rate today. Psychologists suggest that there are a range of factors that provide a person's sense of well-being. Where are you on this list?

You feel in control of your life **(control)** . . . .

You feel healthy and well **(well-being)**. . . . .

You get enjoyment from your life **(enjoyment)** . . . .

You have a sense of gratitude and thankfulness **(gratitude)**. . . . .

Work provides something other than money **(vocation)**. . . . .

You know what's important and you prioritize time for those things **(importance)**. . . . .

You feel connected, not isolated **(connection)**. . . . .

You feel good about yourself **(self-esteem)** . . . .

Give each one of these areas a score between 1 and 10 and this will help you to look more deeply at your life and where you could begin to change areas in order to improve your sense of well-being. Of course these elements will change in your life at different times of change and uncertainty, that is only natural, however, it's a good exercise to do when you need to work out where your stress may be coming from and then it will help you address this area.

Make a decision to become healthy and invest your time now into how you can achieve this. Having good health and well-being is the key to your success in life and that has a direct effect on those you care about too. Do it for yourself and do it for them!

Boost your mental well-being

Which areas did you score high/low on?

Which areas need attention?

Where will improvements make the biggest difference to your life?

What do you need to work on? What are the priority areas for you?
What actions are you prepared to commit to in order to make improvements?
What can you do now and/or in the longer term?
Who could help? Where could you get support?
What do you do when you get stressed out?

Now make your own list here of the 4 main things you do when you feel stressed out:

- ....
- ....
- ....
- ....

Move away from negativity

Do people choose to stay unhappy or negative? We all know people who, no matter what is happening in their lives, always seem to focus on the doom and gloom! Even when things are looking up, they focus on being negative about themselves or negative about those around them or the world they live in. The question is "Why?" Well, if you think about it, a person who is negative usually gets a lot of attention for their complaining and moaning and people get drawn into sympathizing with them and constantly trying to reassure them that everything will be all right! Are you smiling now? Because you probably know someone like this and often feel like saying "Stop complaining and just get on with it". The problem is this person may well be stuck in his or her own negative comfort zone and why would they want to change, when they get so much attention?

Challenge the comfort zone!

Remember this, **YOU** have all the resources inside you to help yourself change things for the better, all you need to do is understand, acknowledge and then take responsibility for yourself in order to move forward again. Here is how you start!

Adopt a healthy lifestyle

If we eat a healthy diet, exercise regularly and ensure we get adequate rest our body is better able to cope with stress when it occurs. It's a fact!

Learn to say NO

Know when to say no and do not take on too much. We cause ourselves a great deal of stress because we do not like to say no to people. We like people to like us and don't like letting people down, so often we take on more than we should. Allow yourself to be assertive and learn to say **NO** without upsetting or offending people, start with small steps and make it part of a daily habit. If you feel stressed by having to say no then the chances are you don't want to say yes but you tell yourself "If I don't say yes I will feel guilty" – right? So don't feel guilty, change your behavior and see what happens! Start today and learn to say what you mean!

Determine what causes you stress

Identify what causes you to become stressed and then try to change your behavior to reduce it; again start with small steps – one thing at a time. Use the techniques shown in this book and keep a diary to track your feelings – the more aware you are of your stress levels, the faster you will be able to deal with it.

Avoid unnecessary conflict

Don't be too argumentative. Is it really worth the stress? Look for the win-win situations. Look for a solution to a dispute where both parties can achieve a positive outcome. Try to find the positive and focus on what you would like to experience.

Manage your time more effectively

We waste a lot of time doing unimportant tasks. Prioritize your day and do the important jobs first. The unimportant ones can wait, and often they will disappear completely leaving you time to do other things. Also, do not put off the unpleasant tasks; you can guarantee that every time you think about them you feel guilty and that causes negative feelings about yourself, causing unnecessary stress.

Recharge your batteries

You will perform in every area of your life much better after a break and easily make up the time you use relaxing. When you begin to feel stressed allow yourself a few minutes to switch off, go for a walk, make a cup of tea, but stop what you are doing and give yourself that much needed time to let the pressure off. You don't have to be superman or superwoman, just be yourself and be kind to that mind and body you own!

Why not pin a post-it note on your PC or in the house, maybe on the bathroom mirror, where you will notice it and spell out the words in big letters......HAVE I TAKEN A BREAK TODAY?

Creating energy and vitality

Coach the life and vitality into your life with **The 8 step challenge.** Try this for 8 days and see the results for yourself!

Step 1 – Breathing

Breathing in oxygen gently yet deeply at the start of each day will really energize you; it will only take a few minutes, but it is vital to start off your day in a positive mindset. Taking a few moments to yourself to breathe in and out deeply is about looking after yourself from the moment you wake and before you go into your day with all the demands it may take from you. It's a way of reminding yourself that you are important, that you want balance and to feel happy.

Simply stand in a space where you can lift your arms high and with your feet knee width apart, breath in deeply through your nose and gently lift your arms high above your head; count 1 as you raise your arms, hold the breath for a count of 4 and then lower your arms counting for 2 and breathing out – that's 1-4-2. Now repeat this 4 times and each time you repeat concentrate on your breath, keeping it gentle, easy and flowing. It is not a test or race, the idea is to focus your mind on yourself and your body for a few moments each day.

When you get into the routine of doing this, then you can do it for longer and at any time during the day when your energy is slowing down or you feel a little stressed; it's all about your taking control of how you feel. Of course practice in the fruit and vegetable aisle at the supermarket or your open plan office might bring a smile to a few faces!

Step 2 – Water

Water is a really easy one. Our bodies are made up of 70% water and when we don't have enough hydration, our body slows down, our internal systems that digest our food become sluggish and this can affect our mind, which in turn can effect our emotions; we can feel tired, get headaches and feel generally slower with no energy. All it takes is to keep an eye on how much water we take in. We tend to drink tea and coffee without thinking, but simply adding in a few glasses or handy bottles of water as you go about during the day, will lift your energy levels and give you a boost. Try it for just a couple of days and you will notice an instant difference.

Step 3 – Exercise

There are so many types of exercise the list is endless, the important thing to remember is choose something you really enjoy and like doing, it could be dancing or swimming or cycling, whatever it is, you decide and make a commitment to start today. Don't worry about being proficient, just enjoy taking the first step and give it 4 to 6 weeks to experience the benefits.

I wanted to lose weight many years ago and set my goal to get fit and lose 56lbs in 1 year. I decided to take up running, but I wasn't fit enough to run and needed to start with little manageable steps. I bought myself some basic running shoes and went for a 1 mile walk to see how it felt; I was pleased that I'd made the first effort and done it, the next goal was another small step, this time to walk 1 mile twice a week and I managed that too. It felt great to get out of the house, away from all the things that were on my mind and breathe the fresh air, move my body and most of all – give myself some much needed time out just for myself.

After a month of keeping up my walking routine, I set my next small goal and began jogging a bit on the 1 mile walk and then a month later increased it to 3 times a week. I was really beginning to feel the difference and my energy levels and spirits were lifting; I noticed that I was becoming more toned and didn't get tired anymore after my walks and the jogging was slowly helping to shift the weight. I sometimes felt self conscious going out in my running clothes and thought people must be looking at me and I'm not running very fast, all sorts of things go through your head when you don't feel very confident, but I told myself 'at least I am out here making an effort and I should be proud of myself not embarrassed.'

There were times I felt so tired and it was cold and raining outside, I just wanted to stay in the warm and not bother, but I made a little chart on the calendar of the progress I was making and I would look at that again and it would keep me focused, so I would keep going. I made myself laugh when I was out on my jogging path, I would need to walk when I got tired and out of breath, but when I saw a car coming along in the distance I would start to jog again, so I would look good and impress people with my fitness!

It did take time, but I reached my end goal and step by step I finally became a runner and lost the weight as I combined exercising 3 times a week and eating a good balance of nutritional food. After 1 year I ran a half marathon, had lost all the weight and I felt amazing. I really did feel like a different person and I was so proud of myself, it was a goal I had achieved literally step by step – I would go out for my run and feel so proud and good about myself; no one had done this for me, it was my achievement, I had made all the effort and you know what – the success was all mine, that felt great.

Running became a passion for me, I set up a local running group and 6 years after taking up my first goal to walk a mile, I ran a marathon, it was one of the most amazing experiences of my life and something I would never ever have imagined possible for me in the past. As my family and friends said to me, it's amazing what you can do when you make a decision that you want something and then take it one step at a time. That's exactly what I did, it started with me putting a post-it note on my fridge to buy some cheap training shoes (that was the very first step) and ended after many, many small steps with one of the greatest achievements I've made in my life crossing the finishing line of the marathon race. I proved to myself that a dream of being able to do something is possible when you break it down into little steps and don't give up!

Don't allow yourself to be put off by feeling overwhelmed by your life goals. The thing to remember is it takes lots and lots of those small steps; when you break down the big goal into bite size steps you move forward little by little and you take away the fear of failing the big goal, because you move forward with your small goals staying on course to achieve the end result. So whatever your exercise goal, be gentle with yourself and start the journey – then go step by step!

(Please seek expert medical advice first if you have any concerns about your health or exercising.)

Step 4 – Food glorious food

Here are some of the tried and tested elements to enjoying your food and keeping it healthy.

- Eat plenty of fruit and vegetables.

- Eat a balanced diet to ensure you get enough nutrition.

- Eat when you are relaxed – not on the go and rushing.

- Eat comfortable amounts.

- Eat organic as much as possible.

- Eat well before the time you retire.

Step 5 – Direct your mind

Use your mind to think positively about yourself and your life in order to create happy feelings instead of stress and negativity; think of solutions to problems and ask problem-solving questions; think about what you eat and how you live your life and take action to change old habits and patterns of behavior; become disciplined with yourself.

Step 6 – Support yourself

Look after yourself and this will support you in the 8-step challenge.

Take some time to rest and if possible get some sunshine, have a massage or do something gentle and nurturing for yourself; what's more, it doesn't have to cost money to support yourself – getting enough sleep, enjoying a walk in the park or just sitting still and relaxing with the newspaper or your favorite magazine or book; you must give yourself time out, you do deserve this you know and if you don't do it for yourself no one else can.

Step 7 – Watch the fats and oils

Keep a diary of the fat and oil you use in the first few days of the challenge, or just reduce your intake of fat and oil by half, give yourself a budget of butter, oil or fat for the 8 days and make it last. Try mixing water and oil in a cooking sprayer – you can buy these in most cook shops and this will automatically reduce your fat and oil intake.

Step 8 – Hidden addictions

Food and drinks containing high amounts of sugar, salt and vinegars can become addictive to the taste buds and too much of them may impact on your health. Cutting out these things for 8 days will enable you to see and taste the difference in your food and drinks, which will help you realize how good food tastes without all the high amounts of sugar, salt and vinegar!

Sarah's story

Sarah came to me for coaching after she had been building up her business for a number of years. She said her dream of being a business woman and the happiness she once felt now felt like it was all about paying the bills and more like a job than a business she was passionate about. She was tired and fed up, with lots of negative emotions and almost ready to give it all up.

When we uncovered what Sarah really valued in her life, which was actually time with her family and feeling fit and healthy – she had always been a great sporty person before she started her business. It became clear that Sarah's business only fulfilled some of her values, which included independence, security, adventure and fun, but left virtually no quality time for her family and to spend time on being healthy and fit.

Once Sarah could see more clearly that she needed to balance these values in her life in order to be happy and that her work was not a negative, but she had let it take over too much of her life, then all the other important areas of her life soon began to shout out to her for attention and she needed to find a solution to incorporate them back into her life.

We got to work right away on rebalancing her time, getting her organized with every bit of her working day and finding creative ways to fit in time for the family and getting fit. It took a few weeks of adjustment and being scheduled, but it totally paid off. Sarah now loves her business more than ever, she has energy and has even expanded her business. Most of all she loves the time spent with family, its quality time for her and she has managed to combine exercise with them too, so they all benefit now.

Sarah promised herself one afternoon a month to take a few hours out and look at whether she was still managing a balance in her life. If it looks like the business is taking over again, she takes stock and changes things if she needs to. It works and she is very much happier knowing she can make better choices.

Summary

- Well-being is about your whole life, mind, body and spirit as well as the obvious physical element of feeling healthy and fit.

- If you have a good balance in all areas of your life it will increase your feeling of well-being.

- No amount of money or material assets will give you a perfect sense of well-being if you neglect areas like relationships and health.

- Your well-being is unique and different from the next person. Understand what that is and strive to achieve this each day.

- Visualize your good health and well-being; it will make it easier to achieve when you believe and see it is possible.

- Your body and mind are a reflection of how well you feel about your life. For positive change look honestly at your life.

- Pressure and stress are a part of life. Learning to say No to things takes the pressure off when you really need to.

- Unhealthy amounts of pressure turn into stress and if ignored take their toll on your health and affect how happy and successful you can be.

- Managing your stress and finding ways to de-stress is the key, whether it's a nice long walk, reading a book or simply getting away from the PC.

- Knowing what your stress triggers are will help you to support yourself and take action to relax before the stress builds into negative amounts.

- Being around positive people and not getting pulled into negative conversation will keep you motivated and not stressed.

- Laughing is a great stress reliever.

Relationships & Communication

" *A great place to meet is on equal terms.* **"**

Anon

Chapter 6
Relationships & Communication

Understanding ourselves is the key to understanding others; when we learn to be open and honest about ourselves then it allows others to do the same in return. A great relationship is one when we feel comfortable about being ourselves, feel most alive and that we are learning, developing and growing as a person, so it makes sense that the way we communicate with each other is an important element of understanding in all our relationships.

Good communication is at the heart of every successful relationship, it allows people to express themselves, educate others and inspire. There are no limits to the opportunities to practice and expand your communication skills. Being a good communicator is key to success in life and you don't have to be a speech maker; you are communicating even before you open your mouth or put pen to paper, so being aware of the signals you're sending out, the way you look, your body language, and your words all have an impact.

Assess your communication skills

Take a moment to look at how you currently communicate and this will create a better awareness for you and therefore help you to make better choices if you want to improve this area of your life.

Q. When other people are talking to you what are you most likely to do:

A. Give them my full attention and remain silent.

B. Listen and repeat back what they said.

C. Start thinking about my own things I need to do.

Q. How do you feel when you have to say no:

A. I find it one of the hardest things to do.

B. It usually takes me some thought to get it right.

C. I have no problem saying no and meaning it.

Q. When you have to confront someone about an important issue:

A. I get someone else to do it for me.

B. I do it face to face, but get someone to support me if necessary.

C. I do it and get the job over and done with.

Q. How do you feel about talking to large groups:

A. I find it very uncomfortable and don't want to do it.

B. I am happy to do it, provided I feel prepared.

C. I love doing it and embrace the opportunity.

Mostly As

You're more of a listener than a talker and may lack a certain amount of confidence when it comes to speaking out for yourself. You see communication as important but not an essential tool for your own progress. Ask yourself if you would benefit from improving your communication and how your life would improve if you did; write down your thoughts here:

. . . .
. . . .
. . . .
. . . .

Mostly Bs

You understand that good communication is important and you try to prepare and plan so that you express yourself as clearly and effectively as possible. However, you may follow a style of communicating that is structured and if you haven't ticked any Cs at all, then it may be that you are a good mediator but hesitate to project your own message to others. Ask yourself if you would benefit from expressing what you feel is important to others and how this might have a positive impact on your life; write down your thoughts here:

. . . .
. . . .
. . . .
. . . .

Mostly Cs

You are confident and forthright and feel very much at ease with the idea of being yourself and expressing yourself clearly to others. However, true communication is a two-way exchange of ideas. Could your forthrightness be blocking out the opportunity for others to express themselves to you? Might you be ignoring those opportunities or be failing to seek the opinions and attitudes of others? You might want to encourage feedback from others to help you build their positive ideas and opinions into your own communication; it's all about a win-win opportunity.

Being a good listener

Are you a good listener? If you can't see how listening is going to help you express yourself to others, then you might need to listen more than others! Whether your goal is to get others to agree, make yourself heard, instruct or motivate others, then communication is the key, however, many problems occur from failure to communicate, leading to misunderstandings and then mistrust. This is usually caused by a failure to listen – a fundamental element of communication. If you want to influence people, you first need to know how they think, and good listening skills will help you to achieve what you want.

Positive communication

1. Listen actively to others, stop what you are doing and concentrate on what they are saying.

2. Turn off your cell phone!

3. Show the person you have made time to listen to them.

4. Face the person and turn your body towards them.

5. Maintain eye contact with them and nod your head if you agree.

6. Ask questions which show you are listening and want to know more.

7. Clarify and confirm any mixed messages you may be picking up.

8. State your opinions or views **only** when they have finished!

Negative communication. Don't:

- Allow your mind to get distracted or day dream – it will show!

- Interrupt people when they are talking.

- Jump in and finish their sentence.

- Look at the clock or your watch all the time.

Interrupting a person when they speak suggests you lack the time or the patience to hear someone out and this means you will never really hear what the person is saying to you, or worse that you don't think they are worth listening to!

Understand the impact of your negative or positive state of mind on your relationships. Do you live in fear and worry about things or are you positive and relaxed and comfortable in the right now? Try this out – next time you have a conversation with someone close to you, your partner, a friend, your child or your own parent, listen to the words you say and the way you speak to them. Catch yourself talking and what you are talking about, do most of your sentences start with 'I' or 'my' or do you ask 'how' 'when' or 'why' questions? Often a person who is focused on themselves controls the conversation with their need to discuss everything relevant to them, their opinions and needs. If you met someone like that and had a conversation with them, would you enjoy that? Would you tell them how they sound? Probably not – the point is, try to recognize how you behave and it will shine light on the way you could improve your relationships.

Speak to people

It might sound really obvious, but there is nothing as pleasant as a cheerful word of greeting, whether it be to the postman or to a grumpy teenager who is at the 'grunt only' phase of life. You might even raise an eyebrow or two in work. You know the saying: "I used to wake up grumpy, but now I let him (or her) sleep in!"

Eating and talking at the same time?

Don't forget to stop and chat over food or a meal! It might sound obvious but we are all in such a hurry these days, we all like to share and be heard, it makes our lives more connected. So turn the television and computers off when you can and sit around a table, ask questions of each other and listen, just the usual day to day stuff, that makes our worlds go round.

Smiling is free

Smiling takes 14 muscles and yet it takes 72 to frown, so how about smiling at the stressed mother with a crying child in the supermarket or remember a time when you benefited from a stranger smiling at you! Make a point of smiling at people and see the response you get – it will lift your spirits and help you practice a positive attitude. By the way – don't let the really grumpy faces who refuse to smile back put you off, there is always someone very happy to receive a smile and it costs nothing to make another person happy!

Smiling

Smiling is infectious
You catch it like the flu,
When someone smiled at me today
I started smiling too.
I passed around the corner
And someone saw me grin,
When he smiled I realized
I'd passed it on to him.
I thought about the smile
And realized its worth
A single smile like mine
Could travel round the earth.
If you feel a smile begin
Don't leave it undetected
Let's start an epidemic quick
and get the world infected.

Medicine for the soul

Did you know that people who are depressed or ill can feel better and recover more quickly by laughing and smiling? A smile releases serotonin, a powerful neurotransmitter that makes us feel better.

What's in a name?

It's like music to a person's ears when they hear the sound of their own name and it shows that you are making a conscious effort to be interested. It's the simplest way of being meaningful to another person, so make a point of saying their name back to them in conversation; it will help them to feel more comfortable with you and more positive towards you.

Be generous with praise

Great communication in any relationship is based on trust and a few ill-chosen words that are critical of a person can be devastating to any relationship. However, someone who is known for being encouraging is always popular. So if you are not generally the type of person who gives praise to others, start to do it in little ways where you can and you will notice not just a difference in the way people see you and think of you, but it feels good to know you are helping others with encouragement rather than negativity.

QUICK T!P

As the saying goes "If you don't have anything positive to say – then say nothing at all!"

" If you do what you've always done, you will always get what you have always got. "

Anon

3 sides to any controversy

Your side, the other person's, and the right one!

There are some battles that are just not worth undertaking, and others that are just not worth winning – even if you are right. Think about the long-term effect and the amount of energy it takes to battle over something negative. Ask yourself first if it will be worth all that effort and what will be the reward to you. If the reality shows that you don't actually win anything other than you confirming to yourself that you can win arguments, then is it really worth the point – or would your time be better spent concentrating on your happiness and goals?

Sorry seems to be the hardest word...

"I'm sorry" may at times feel like the hardest words to say to someone – but they are **THE** most powerful. It might feel like you are being strong and sticking to your principles or opinions by not saying sorry, but when you say those words and mean it, you are released from negativity and empowered with positive emotions. Try it next time you don't feel like saying sorry and feel how it releases feelings of fear, anxiety and worry. Like anything in life, the more you practice the better you get.

A sense of humor

Some people are just naturally gifted with a sense of humor that makes other people laugh and it helps put people at ease. For you to develop your own sense of humor, look at the things about yourself that make you smile. Learn to allow yourself the opportunity of not always being perfect, take the pressure off and have a giggle at the things that didn't always go right, look at the other side of the situation and find something funny in it. This will help you to relax about yourself and develop your confidence to feel OK with all elements of who you are.

Speaking with confidence

Develop your confidence to communicate in work and relationships by joining a local public speaking club. They offer a supportive environment in which you can build up your public speaking and leadership skills. These clubs are friendly and help you in the art of speaking, listening, and thinking on your feet, skills that will enhance your self-confidence and personal growth, not just for work, but in all your relationships, helping you to become more assertive in a non-threatening environment.

Body language speaks volumes

Did you know it takes less than 30 seconds for a person to make a decision about another person when they first see them? Before that person has even said a word! That's because we all read each other through our facial expressions and body language as well as the voice.

In order to communicate well in all relationships it is said that you must first be aware of your emotions and learn how to control those emotions, because other people will be reading these emotions and making a judgement.

Assessing the emotions of others

If you are intimidated, angry, afraid or resentful your ability to communicate and motivate others will be limited. Being aware of how you feel and taking responsibility for those feelings is the first step and then you will realize how you are affecting others. Think about what you want to achieve and imagine how you will achieve this by feeling negative towards that person; now imagine being calm and positive to help you communicate clearly and ask yourself which way of communicating is really going to get your message across and achieve the result you want.

Negative body language

Do you do any of these things when you feel angry, resentful, afraid? How would you feel if someone was doing them to you?

- Avoiding eye contact.

- Turning towards the door to go.

- Checking the time frequently.

- Folding arms across the chest.

- Scratching the back of the neck.

- Looking downwards.

Be aware of how your body is communicating, and by changing your body language, you will begin to feel differently inside about your emotions. You will be more aware and in control.

Building rapport

Building rapport with another person is part of great communication. When you are in good rapport with someone, you may have the same sense of humor, like the same things and feel connected from the start. It's a great feeling and yet it happens on a subconscious level. Actually what you are doing is subconsciously recognizing that you like this person and what they are saying interests you, without realizing you will automatically begin to mirror their behavior in a similar way. If you were to look at yourself in rapport with another person, it would look like one person in a mirror reflecting back the same gestures. A great way to observe this is in a restaurant. Look at the couples around you and the ones who look interested and attracted to each other will be in rapport. Watch their body language, the way they sit, how they cross their legs and their gestures which will imitate each other's without them knowing they are doing it.

Facing up to friction

Dealing with friction in relationships, wherever they are, either at home or at work will enable you to live with more peace and happiness, create positive energy and help you gain in confidence to be yourself. There will always be difficult people in life but good communication can go a long way towards smoothing the way and removing negativity and misunderstandings.

Learn to face the friction in order to prevent it from escalating, it's vital to acknowledge a problem exists, otherwise it becomes internalized and we can become angry and frustrated, letting off steam with friends and partners when it's nothing to do with them.

Four minute fix

If someone is annoying you and you want to avoid a confrontation – try this:

■ Ask yourself whether this person is reacting to you because they perceived something negative coming from you.

■ Suggest to this person that you may have done something to upset them. Or have you rubbed them up the wrong way without knowing?

■ Encourage them to point out exactly what their problem is with you.

■ Listen to what they say and repeat their point back to them for clarity.

This will only take a few minutes, but from this point you will both feel better understood and be able to make a more positive decision about how to feel about each other; go on be brave and give it a try – it works!

Sharing feelings

It's easy to bluntly tell a person what you think, what you want or need them to do, however, it can lead to that person feeling defensive and responding negatively to you. How you phrase your words will affect the response you receive to what you have said.

- Think about what you want to express and state the facts.

- Think about how you feel about this.

- Consider what is causing you to feel like this.

- Think about the outcome you want.

Practice here with a situation you want to address:

For example

- Talking to my partner about money issues!

- Talking to my teenager about behavior issues!

- Talking to my boss about a problem at work!

- Talking to my parent about health concerns!

There could be any number of things you really need to sort out and so far have not done – right! OK so do this exercise and come out with a plan of how you will tackle it in a positive way.

What is it that you need to express? Just the facts – write them down:

. . . .
. . . .
. . . .
. . . .
. . . .
. . . .

How do you feel about it? For example, it's making you worry, feel angry, unhappy etc and how is this affecting you? For example, not sleeping or taking your energy and you feel tired? Write them down:

. . . .
. . . .

. . . .
. . . .
. . . .
. . . .

Think about the kind of positive outcome you want for both yourself and the other person. Write it down:

. . . .
. . . .
. . . .
. . . .
. . . .
. . . .

Think about what will happen if you don't express yourself. What will happen a week from now, a month or a year from now? Is that what you really want? Write it down so that it becomes a motivation for change and action:

. . . .
. . . .
. . . .
. . . .
. . . .
. . . .

Decide when and where is the best place to talk and make a commitment to get it sorted out and focus on your solution and positive outcome. What action are you going to take? Write it down.

. . . .
. . . .
. . . .
. . . .
. . . .
. . . .

Now you have a constructive plan to help you discuss what you want and if necessary take it with you when you have your conversation, it will help you stay on track to explain all the elements of what you think and it will also show the person how serious you are about wanting them to understand what you think, feel and need.

Creating a brilliant relationship

Take some time to write down a list of the things you must have in a partner to feel happy and then circle the ones that are an absolute priority and a MUST HAVE and then look at the ones you would like, but could live without or make a compromise on. Doing this will help you to be clear about what you want and it will allow you to be honest with yourself. It will enable you to communicate these important elements from the start of any relationship.

Being honest about what you need and then being able to recognize that these needs are not being met earlier rather than later in any relationship, will help you make better decisions rather than hoping that things will change on their own. You can take responsibility for creating a brilliant relationship through talking about what you really need.

How to know what you need

Start with looking at what you value, what is important to you as an individual and you can use the chapter on 'Finding your Passion' to clarify what you value and who you are. From this point you will be able to imagine a relationship with someone who has the same values! Look back over your past relationships and look at the values you both shared, were there conflicts around areas where you both took a different perspective? If you are in a relationship that might have conflicts, work out what you both need and whether these needs are being met, and look at whether it would be possible to achieve.

Write it down

Working through a difficult time in any relationship is hard. None of us like confrontation usually and we don't like admitting we feel sad or hurt easily too. So when things go wrong in relationships its not easy and we often feel bad because we are not dealing with it and this makes us feel more hurt and sad and that brings us down emotionally. It's a vicious circle though because when we feel like this it inhibits our ability to communicate with confidence about who we are and what we want.

For some people this lack of confidence to communicate honestly about their emotions in their relationships can go on for years and have a very damaging effect, to the point where things explode and then it feels too late to fix it.

Coaching many people (including myself!) to be honest with our emotions and be able to express ourselves is so important. So many people make excuses to themselves that it doesn't matter and that things will get better on their own, but we all need to feel loved and respected and accepted for who we are.

With this in mind I help my clients to write down what they are feeling and why and what they would like to feel. It might sound simplistic and in a way it is, but there is something about writing it down to yourself that makes it real and you can be more objective about it. This then leads to a feeling of empowerment, you can see and understand who you are and why you feel the way you do. Awareness to help us move forward is the key, loving and respecting ourselves is the first step and then we can share this attitude with others and it does make it easier the more you practice it.

When we accept ourselves and what we truly need and want and can express that to others, we do not become sad and negative, we are empowered and feel free. It's a great feeling and worth taking the time to write down.

Summary

- Understanding yourself is the most important way of understanding others.

- Feeling comfortable with another person and being able to express yourself and how you feel is the key to successful relationships.

- You don't have to be a speech maker to be a great communicator. Tone of voice, the words you use, and your body language all have an impact.

- Learning to be a great listener is a fantastic skill to help you improve communication and understand yourself better.

- Preparing and writing down what you want to say will give you confidence and keep you focused on expressing the key issues.

- When you are having a conversation, turn your cell phone off; it shows you respect the other person and that the conversation is important to you.

- Maintaining good eye contact and nodding your head in agreement is a clear way of showing interest and understanding of what is being communicated to you.

- If you feel tempted to jump in and finish off other people's sentences, reflect on why you need to control the conversation. Is it a positive way of communicating or does it disempower the other person?

- Using the word 'I' a lot in conversation shows that you are unable to listen. Using 'you' and 'we' is far more respectful and positive.

- Smiling and just saying Hello is the easiest and most wonderful way to cheer up someone, and it has an amazing way of spreading a good feeling to others.

Work
& Money

" *Finish each day and be done with it. You have done what you could. Some blunders and absurdities no doubt crept in; forget them as soon as you can. Tomorrow is a new day; begin it well and serenely and with too high a spirit to be encumbered with your old nonsense.* **"**

Ralph Waldo Emerson

Chapter 7
Work & Money

Although work and money are connected, they also stand alone as important elements of everyone's life. How you decide to live your life is based heavily around the sort of work you do or would like to do, being happy in your work is one thing, however, being in control of your money is another. If you don't feel you are in control of this area in your life it can spoil all the hard work and energy you put into the things you value. For example, being in debt or having money worries can cause stress, which can affect your health, your relationships, your confidence and judgement. So it makes sense to get to grips with your money situation and also to look at how you can improve your work life.

Taking small, yet manageable steps to achieve your work and money goals will help you develop your confidence and empower you to live the life you want. The first step is to assess where you are financially and even if it appears negative, at this point you can start to create the solutions to improve your situation. Awareness is the key.

So whether having a lot or just a little money is important to you individually, having awareness and taking control of your work life and your finances is a vital part of feeling happy in your life, after all most of us spend most of our lives working so it makes sense to get it right. Money may give us more choices, but if you don't have a clear picture of what your financial situation is, then how can you feel confident about any decisions or choices you may want to take in life, because you won't know where you will end up.

Working for different reasons

People work for different reasons, what are your reasons? Let's explore in more detail and set goals to improve this area of your life.

1. To meet other people and have company.

2. To earn money, which gives more choices.

3. To experience a sense of fulfillment.

4. To have a level of status and significance.

5. To make a difference and have a sense of vocation.

6. To keep busy and occupied.

Why do you work? It could be one answer or a combination of reasons.

Write down your answer here:

. . . .
. . . .
. . . .
. . . .

Complementing who you are

Finding the right career is all about finding something that complements your natural strengths and allows you to develop and explore yourself in a way that suits you. Take a moment to think about the ideas you had when you first thought about what sort of job you would like to do, and remember what made you feel excited and filled you with enthusiasm. These feelings are fuelled by your inner self, the way you see the world, what you value and how you would like to experience life, so it stands to reason that finding a job or career that allows you to be who you are will make you feel happy and help you develop your strengths as that person.

The right or wrong job for me

What if your job not only paid the bills, but also made you happier and more successful? Well, now it can as long as you know what the right job for you really is. Don't feel pushed into doing any job in order to make enough money to pay the bills, take some time or get some expert advice to help you find a job that will enhance your life beyond money. Taking the time to do this will help you stay true to who you are and what makes you happy as a person, by understanding what you value, you will be able to know which direction to go in when it comes to finding a career or job. *(Refer to Chapter 3: Finding your Passion.)*

My ideal job is?

Do you feel deeply that your work is right for you? Answer **Yes** or **No.**

Do you feel frustrated or irritated with an aspect of your work? Answer **Yes** or **No.**

So do your answers make you question what you are doing currently in your job? What would you ideally like to do? Imagine your ideal job now and here are some questions to help you think it through. Write down your thoughts next to each one.

What would the job entail?

. . . .
. . . .
. . . .
. . . .

Is the job full time or part time and why?

. . . .
. . . .
. . . .
. . . .

How much money would you want to earn?

. . . .
. . . .

Where would you work, outside, inside office, at home?

. . . .
. . . .

What qualifications, training, and experience would you need?

. . . .
. . . .
. . . .
. . . .
. . . .
. . . .
. . . .

Would you want to work for yourself or for others?

. . . .
. . . .

How far away from home would you work?

. . . .
. . . .

Would you need or want to move or live somewhere different?

. . . .
. . . .

Would you want to manage other people?

. . . .
. . . .

Great, now you have designed your ideal job, so take a look at your job description and ask yourself "If I saw this job advertised, what would I need to do in order to consider sending off my details and applying for this role/job?" or "If I was creating this as a job or business for myself do I have everything in place to do this?" Which areas of myself do I need to improve for it to become a reality? Do I need new skills, develop my character/attitude, qualifications and do I need specific experience? From this point you have a goal and you can start to take the first steps to moving forward towards your ideal job.

What are you going to do first? It may be talk to someone, do some research or get more information on your ideas – write it here:

. . . .
. . . .
. . . .
. . . .

Where would I like to be in 5 years' time?

This is one of those questions that gets you thinking. Where you would like to be and where you are now may be two different places, but without having your goals clear in your mind, then you will be open to all sorts of influences and may end up in exactly the same position in 5 years' time. So have a plan of what you would like to achieve and how your life will look in 5 years' time; don't forget to look at all the things you value and the areas of your life and make sure they are included (refer to the Chapters Finding your Passion and Setting Personal Goals). This will help you when it comes to deciding on where you want to work, what you want to do, who you want to work with and how you could achieve it. By being honest with yourself first, you can start to move closer to your work and money goals.

Don't be put off by change

One of the easiest ways of giving up on your hopes and dreams of an ideal job or career is FEAR! Don't let it put you off with the thoughts of having to make changes to your life. It is important to take responsibility for any changes you make and take into consideration how it may effect other people, however, you have one life and it can sometimes feel easier to give into what others may need, rather than what you need in order to be yourself. Think it through, be sensitive to others, but don't talk yourself out of being your best, you have one life – make it a happy one!

Giving yourself rewards

Allow yourself the time and opportunity to appreciate how hard you have worked and what you have achieved in your life already. Sometimes it's all too easy to be in such a rush to progress and improve oneself, that you don't stop to look at how well you are doing and how far you have come. Look back through your diary over the past year or years and taking a colored pen, mark all the dates that you felt you achieved something positive, had a great experience or did something positive for your life.

Think about your family, your job, your friends, things you changed for the better, things you achieved which have helped you in some way. Mark them all, because they are all positive, and reward yourself with something nice to remind you of how well you are doing. Whatever it may be, it's about you letting yourself deserve the reward and feeling good about your personal successes; they will motivate and inspire you to keep progressing.

Time management

Taking the 'time' to look at how you use your 'time' will help you to work and live more efficiently, allowing you more free time to relax and re-energize and do all the other things you enjoy apart from earning money and working.

Take a look at your typical working week, it doesn't matter what you do, if you go to work, if you look after your family, if you have retired, the point is to use your time to get the most out of your life.

Break down the week into the seven days and write a list of the things that you have to do, and the time it takes out of your week, then write in the things you would like to do and the things that you could fit in after that.

Now take a look at this week. If it doesn't change are you going to be happy with it and will it be a positive way of living your life? Do you have enough time for all the things you know are important to you or do you have too much time and need to be constructive? The main thing to recognize with this exercise is how you feel about the way you currently manage your time and then once you have this awareness, take responsibility to make small steps – one thing at a time – to allow enough time for all of your needs to be met.

Take one area that stands out for you as important because you have not allowed enough time for yourself to enjoy it and think of one thing you could change to manage time for this more effectively.

For example… Family, Friends, Partner, Home, Fun, Social Life, Health, Personal Development, and …Work and Money!

Today I am going to change this area of my life by doing one thing to improve my time management – this will be:

. . . .
. . . .
. . . .
. . . .

Feeling under pressure from work?

Make an appointment with yourself in your own diary to devote at least one or two hours a week to relax by doing an activity that you really enjoy, such as a long walk, a cycle ride, a swim, a massage, reading a great book or a visit to the gym; book it in to your schedule otherwise weeks will go by and although you really wanted to, you never found the time!

Sleep is wonderful

Make getting enough sleep a priority. If you are under extra pressure from work, then getting some early nights will reduce the experience. If you can't sleep, then reflect and write down your successes that day, no matter how small, even a friendly smile to a colleague; realize that being tired will make things seem 100% worse than they are and the pressure could turn into stress!

Last thing at night...

When you have things on your mind about work and you find it hard to get to sleep as all the questions are whizzing around in your head, keep a little notebook and pen on your bedside table and write down your thoughts; this helps to empty your brain onto paper allowing it to feel more relaxed.

Be kind to yourself

Be gentle with yourself, do things you love as often as possible and don't feel guilty. Tell that negative voice in the back of your mind that you do deserve some time out for yourself, otherwise chances are no one else is going to know how much you need it and before you know it weeks, months and even years have gone by and you feel like your life is mainly about work!

Laughing is a tonic

There are days at work and in life, when nothing seems to go right, it just happens sometimes, that's life. However, rather than letting it get you down, try giving yourself a tonic of smiling! To smile and laugh as much as you can will release happy hormones around your body and lift your mood. If you can't do that at work, then try a funny movie to make you giggle and chuckle and get into a positive state of mind. Once you've found something that just makes you giggle because it's so silly, then watch it over again whenever you need to get back to feeling positive, it works!

Take that break

Take at least a ten-minute break each day to ease off from your schedule. You can do this by taking a stroll, coffee break or by doing something equally relaxing. It can be so easy to stay at your computer or working through a lunch break, deadlines to meet and you want to give a good impression. However, no one will stop you from doing this to yourself and when you end up tired and unhappy in your job, feeling overwhelmed and under pressure, who will you blame? You can say NO; you can stop and you can look after yourself.

Stay on course

Having goals and taking responsibility is important, however, don't take yourself or life so seriously that it becomes stressful and you feel compelled to be perfect. Realize that if you fail at something, it is not the end of the world. Smile and know that you and your goals are important and you will dust yourself down and get back on track. Remember there is no such thing as failure – only delayed results!

Who do you spend your time with?

Remember that who you spend your time with is very important, as the saying goes "who you spend time with is who you become", so take a good look around and ask yourself honestly whether you really like the company you keep and do you feel positive being around these people, do you like being around them? For some people it's easy to get into the habit of being critical and negative; keep your distance from negativity, and those people who like to gossip as it can easily pull you in and you may end up feeling drained of energy. Look at how you could be positive in this situation or simply stay away from it. Take action and do one thing that will bring you closer to feeling happier today.

Head in the sand syndrome

Don't bury your head in the sand over money worries or debts. It can help in the short term to ignore something so important, however, eventually it will catch you up and then you will have so much sorting out you will wish you had taken control over it sooner.

So many people feel guilty for not understanding their finances or for getting into financial difficulty, whether it was deliberate or a mistake. One way to move forward and feel happy and free of anxiety is to get someone who can be objective and unemotional to help you FACE IT. It may feel uncomfortable to start with, even embarrassing, but so what, from this point you will be in charge and be able to make better decisions. Remember, whose life is it we are talking about here? Is it your life or has money got all the control? You decide, but remember the longer you ignore it, the less control you have and more work you will have to do to put it right!

Saving money by working at home

It can sometimes be quicker to increase your income by saving some income! How about saving some money by working from home? More and more jobs can be done at home, so look at what you do and see if there is any time you could spend at home doing a job or an element of your existing job, for example emailing, making calls, working on your personal computer with the internet. Could you spend one day working at home? This could save you money on travel, running car costs and stress, whilst giving you more flexibility for other life commitments such as family. Work out how much this would save you over a year and it will add up!

Budgeting money

It will help you to achieve your life goals if you know how much money you really need to live on and how much money you want in order to achieve your hopes and dreams. However, if you spend everything you have each month and don't budget for what you need as your life develops (for example a growing family, moving house, health, new experiences) then it is tempting to borrow money to maintain the lifestyle you want and have the finances to develop your life. That is understandable, however, having a budget that you can monitor will help you to avoid getting into debt and over stretching yourself financially; it will help you to look at what you really need and what you would like and be able to make plans to save money for things rather than borrow, because after all, borrowing is not like the friendly neighbor asking "Can I borrow your lawnmower – mine's broken down?" which is a free gesture; borrowing money involves paying it back – with the interest, which keeps adding up – and 9 times out of 10 you realize it would have been much, much cheaper to save and pay for it in cash!

Time to get it sorted

How much time do you have left in your life to organise your life and sort out areas of your life that need improving? If it's having the job or career you really want or making enough money for the things you would like, then here's a quick and effective way of looking at how much time you have to achieve it!

Work – Money – Life – how much time do I really have?

Take your present age and subtract if from 80 (which is an average age you'll live – if you are 80 already or think you will live to a longer age then choose a greater number). Now multiply it by 12. For example, if you're 42: $80 - 42 = 38 \times 12 = 456$.

This is the number of months you're likely to have left in this life!

How quickly the months go by, so don't delay – start living today!

James's story

James was a very busy executive with a high pressured job. He traveled a lot which took him away from his family and friends, but he loved his job and had worked hard to gain a great position in his company and develop an exciting career.

The problem was that the more he worked the more he earned, but the price was high and the stress that came with it. It was almost like an addiction that he could not control and what had started with genuine intentions to be his best and provide for his family, was now really having a negative effect on his life. Simply put he had work and he had money, but he did not have a life!

Once we looked at how this situation had developed, it helped James to develop a deeper sense of self awareness regarding what his motivations and beliefs were driving him to do regarding his work and what money meant to him. This made a really big difference to James, because he could now make better decisions when it came to the demands on his life from his job.

James realized what was most important to him was to have balance, time for all the things that made him happy. There was no time to enjoy all his hard efforts because he had lost this balance. It didn't take James long to make a few small adjustments and feel the benefit of this, he still had his great job and was secure financially, but he learnt the value of both and where they fitted in to the bigger picture of his life.

When he told me that his little boy said to him one evening that he needed his Daddy and that it was so nice to have him tuck him into bed and read a story once more, James knew he had turned a corner. The work and the money were a source of importance, so that he could enjoy his family and life, not the other way round when it took away his life!

Summary

- Getting to grips with your finances will help you to set goals around work and life.

- Finding work that complements your natural strengths will increase your chances of being happy.

- If you feel frustrated about your job, write down how to use your strengths, skills and abilities to change your situation.

- When choosing work, first ask yourself what you would really like to do and then find a way to achieve it.

- Researching all the possible jobs that exist, particularly on the internet, may turn up an ideal job that you had not considered before.

- Ask yourself where you would like to be in 5 years' time? Look at how work and money fit in with your plans. Write down these goals.

- Goals to increase your income or change your job can all be put off by 'fear'. Take 100% responsibility for the results you want to achieve.

- Stay motivated at work and look back through your diary, highlighting in a bright color all your positive achievements.

- Manage your time and allow yourself a balance of work and time for the other areas of your life.

- A budget for your money will help you to stay in control of your life and increase your confidence and self-worth.

- Pressures of work can lead to stress, so make an appointment with yourself in your own diary for at least two hours a week that is just for you.

- Be more productive and save money by working from home.

Making
a Difference

" Happiness is not achieved by the conscious pursuit of happiness; it is generally the by-product of other activities. "

Aldous Huxley

Chapter 8
Making a Difference

You have taken the time to pick up this book and look at your life and how you could improve it, whether you are looking for motivation, clarity or progress, it is all centered around you! However, this chapter takes you one step closer to finding ways to develop a way of living that naturally causes you to feel happy daily and better still, it will invite you to generate happiness in your life from the heart.

Once you understand who you are and what is important to you by using the tips in the other chapters, you will then be able to consider an important element of living, which is contribution! Making a difference to the life you live in and the one you will leave behind is something we all think about and when you feel this, it gives a person a deep sense of purpose and in return peace, contentment and happiness.

We are all messed up and imperfect – thank God!

Who are you? What do you want? Where are you going in life? All these questions have been asked in the previous chapters, however, remember your imperfections are what make you unique! Everything you decide to do in your life starts and lasts with one simple intention; to make yourself happy and to make other people happy; on the way we all mess up and get it wrong, so give yourself a break. It is understanding all elements of who you are that will help you to see the way forward and know your purpose.

I want to make a difference

We often feel at a loss as to how we can have a positive impact on the world and the people around us. However, feeling helpless can often lead to us feeling useless and unable to know what to do for the best, we question our ability and then give in to negativity too easily. It is possible to enrich and rejuvenate your life with purpose, however, it is important to get rid of the word *apathy* and replace it with *action.* Too much time is spent thinking about what we could do or might do – if only we had more time, if only we had more money, if only we had more energy. So it has to start with ACTION.

Appreciating what you already have!

Firstly, it's good to start with a basic way of looking at the things you have in your life, as all too often we tend to take them for granted. To discover your purpose in life, you need to start with what you have already achieved! It can be too easy to focus on what you haven't got and constantly strive to achieve more and more without taking the time to look at what you already have!

Try taking a reality check and remember something that you are grateful for, remember something that you value in your life right now and how you have worked to make that happen. It could be a relationship, a home, a qualification and job or something you have created and physically built. Take a moment to think about this and how these things don't just happen, everything takes effort, time and thought. We sometimes forget to stop and think how far we have come and what we have already got.

Ask yourself these following basic questions

1.   Does **anyone** love me? . . . . Yes - No

2.   Do I have **somewhere** to live . . . . Yes - No

3.   Do I have **enough** to eat. . . . . Yes - No

4. Do I have **interests** or hobbies I enjoy? . . . . Yes - No

5. Am I **able** to earn a living? . . . . Yes - No

6. Am I able to **look after** myself? . . . . Yes - No

7. Is my **health** reasonably good? . . . . Yes - No

If you get stressed about getting more out of life, then come back to these basics when that happens and remind yourself of what you **do** have and how valuable that is to you. Look after these elements and remember to put things into perspective.

Don't sacrifice your humanity

Having affluence and achievement is all well and good, but if you lose sight of appreciating the good things you already have in life, you may well end up less happy the more you achieve!

How many times do you hear successful people saying "If I had the time to do it all again, I would have taken the time to appreciate my partner, spend more time listening to my children, taking the time to look after my health, go and visit my parents" and so on! We all know that it's easy to get wrapped up in work and other things that we personally enjoy, we even convince ourselves that when it's all done we will take that holiday, visit the grandparents, get home early to have dinner with the kids, etc. Then the time creeps up on us and we have not made time for those things and you know what – those things do matter to us and we deserve to enjoy them, not just FIT them into our busy lives. However, only you can make that decision and make that happen. One life remember!

If you were to think forward in time and imagine your life exactly as it is now – it has just moved forward in time 10 years – would there be anything that you might regret and feel you didn't appreciate along the way?

Write it down here to help you appreciate the here and now!

I have lived on another 10 years and when I look back I wish I'd appreciated…

. . . .
. . . .
. . . .
. . . .
. . . .
. . . .

Learning from our mistakes

Don't be afraid to make mistakes. There is an old saying that people who haven't made mistakes haven't made anything. Allow yourself off the hook here, you know we all make mistakes and the point is to learn and develop positively from them. Ask yourself today, am I holding onto old mistakes that make me feel bad about myself and if so is this going to prevent me from having the life I would like and a sense of purpose that I would really like to feel? If you have, then dump it in the trash right now; it does not serve you any purpose and is spoiling your future happiness.

Use a visualization technique here to help you; find a quiet space and take a few moments to sit in silence, breathe deeply and focus on the thought that you have identified – the one that makes you feel bad about yourself – now consider these 4 things:

What are the facts, just the facts. . . . .

How it makes you feel, just your feelings . . . .

What has this helped you to learn about yourself . . . .

How will you turn that learning into a positive for your life or future – what good are you going to do with what you've learnt? . . . .

If you want to do this exercise, write down the answers to the questions and record them into a digital recorder then play your voice back to yourself in that quiet space – tell yourself how it needs to be!

If you have more than one thought that holds you back, then take the one that scares you the most and hit it head on, get rid of those negative thoughts and keep playing it back to yourself to really tell your inner person the truth – (not that old limiting belief that has held you back – that goes in the trash can right?)

Challenge your negativity

Be aware of any negative thoughts you might be holding about yourself and don't accept them! Challenge them; are they REALLY true, if so what is the evidence? Are you giving yourself a hard time and being highly critical of yourself? When you hear yourself sounding negative, tell yourself to cut it out and be gentle on yourself – tell yourself a positive truth – remember something nice and positive about yourself, something you do that pleases you or that makes others happy, then tell yourself out loud what that is.

Write down a list of things here that you can say to yourself when you feel negativity creeping in.

For example...

Think back to a time you felt really pleased with yourself and had a personal success, take a few moments to allow yourself to remember how it felt and bring those positive feelings back into your mind.

Write those positive feelings down here:

. . . .
. . . .
. . . .
. . . .
. . . .
. . . .
. . . .
. . . .

Stop blaming and start living

The moment you look at who you are and what you want, it can be easy to ignore the elements of your character that you are not entirely comfortable with! If we were all totally honest with ourselves, then all sorts of imperfections would come to mind and it becomes easy to push these thoughts out of the mind and to pretend we don't have them. After all it can feel uncomfortable to admit that we sometimes get it wrong or that we are not always good. Take a moment to consider being honest with yourself about elements of your personality that exist and accept that is who you are sometimes or have been in the past. Stop blaming others for how you feel, when you may have had an influence on these areas of your life, and begin to take responsibility for all elements of who you are, the good, the bad, and the ugly!

It is from this point of truth that you can begin to really start living and being yourself. Accepting yourself and everything that you are is one of the hardest things that people find to do, often because we feel it is impossible to measure up for those important people in our life that we love and only want to show them we are worthy to be loved and liked. In order to be a person that is content and at peace with who they are, the only way is to accept yourself, try to be your best and take responsibility for what you do. It's a daily challenge and YOU WILL get it wrong, that is life and we are all imperfect, make mistakes and don't want to feel bad about ourselves, however, the day you decide to accept all of who you are, that is the day you begin to move forward and feel free to improve and be your best. Only you can do that for you, it takes courage, but it's the best gift you can ever give yourself and will have a fundamental improvement on your emotional well-being.

In need of a little inspiration

Ever see a movie or hear a story of someone who had courage or achieved great things with their life? Maybe a rags-to-riches story or an amazing sporting achievement that stands out because the person overcame enormous physical or emotional obstacles in their desire to succeed. Take up reading some good uplifting books, there are excellent biographies and great self-help books that keep your mind motivated and inspired to stay positive. Look for the common denominator in all these stories, what element is it that makes people want to strive and challenge themselves to succeed against such odds?

I think you will find that it is the amount of 'suffering' they endure and this suffering increases their desire to fight back and through suffering they tap into a powerful human inner strength, which enables them to connect to the most basic but often precious elements of life. They learn from this place of suffering about who they are, what really matters to them and when they survive that suffering, they automatically have a respect for life that goes beyond anything they ever experienced when life seemed stable, healthy, safe and secure. Read those books or listen to a speaker telling of their experience and tune into this inspiration. You don't have to have suffered to appreciate what matters to you in life, but it is all too easy to focus on what you don't have and forget what you already have and what matters to you in life.

Discovering your purpose

When did you last feel a great sense of happiness and gratitude?

The chances are it was when another person did something special for you, helped you out, gave you love or showed you that you are important in this world. It's natural to want and need this, that's what makes our lives so amazing; we have the ability to create so much happiness in the lives of other people with a really simple concept – love.

So it makes sense that in order to discover your purpose in life, you will realize this when you find the ability to be yourself and show the world who you are, and by loving yourself you will be able to give to and love others.

So here's the question – what opportunities do you have to show the world your love towards others?

Here are some examples to get you thinking:

- Being a loving parent, partner, friend, son, or daughter.

- Giving your time to others.

- Being a kind and caring person.

- Showing compassion to those less fortunate.

- Helping others without wanting in return.

- Looking after yourself, being responsible.

- Having respect and tolerance.

- Developing yourself to be your best.

- Inspiring others to be their best.

- Being encouraging and supportive.

- Being forgiving and understanding.

Then it also stands to reason that you can do these things when you are able to do this for yourself. So...

- Be loving towards yourself, yes this is selfish, it is fundamental if you are to be happy.

- Give time to yourself, take that time out you keep talking about, just do it today.

- Be kind to yourself, stop giving yourself a hard time, be gentle with yourself.

- Show compassion to yourself, you will make mistakes, so love those mistakes too.

- Give help to yourself, don't wait for someone else to do it, you make the effort.

- Take responsibility for yourself, stop making excuses, it's your life 100% yours.

- Respect yourself, stand up for yourself and be proud to do what you said you would.

- Be tolerant with yourself, you are allowed to be individual, be understanding to this.

- Be the best you can be, do not settle, you will always feel most alive if you are your best.

- Be an inspiration to yourself, that's right don't leave it up to others, you can do it too.

- Encourage and support yourself, ask for that help and support, don't be so proud.

- Understand yourself, take the time to learn who you are, like reading this book.

- Forgive yourself, it serves you no purpose other than to hold you back.

- Know your values and live them out daily in your life, in your work and relationships, everything.

- Develop your passion, don't be afraid to show what you love and express yourself.

- Set your personal goals. It will keep you motivated and your happiness levels up.

- Live by contributing to others – it feels fantastic to be able to make a difference to others.

…simple really – to love and you will feel love in return.

Jonathan's story

People often say they want to make a difference, meaning giving or doing something significant and selfless for others.

Jonathan was retired and had the time and wisdom of his years to consider how he could make a difference and why it was important to him. Looking at his experiences and skills, together with his personal values he came up with a lot of ideas and then began testing them out with a bit of research to see how realistic they might be to pursue.

Eventually he settled for a combination of doing the things that he enjoyed on a daily basis being retired, as this made him a happy person to be around and his family would appreciate that! However, he also began a creative project that was non-profit making and could help children with disabilities. This was something he had considered for many years, but simply did not know where to begin with it all, so once he started the project he immediately began to feel excited about it.

From the first day of his project he was so motivated and inspired, that he said he felt 10 years younger with a real sense of purpose, a passion and to know it would make a big difference to others was such a great feeling. The day that the project came to life and he could see what it was doing for the children and their families was fantastic and it has now become a lifelong passion that he has made new friends and begun a whole new chapter in his life.

Jonathan is a great case study of someone that embraced a major change in his life and became aware of his passion to help others and how happy that made him feel. He set goals, which motivated him to take action and resulted in him feeling more alive than he had felt for years – he knew his actions were making others happy!

Summary

- Make a positive difference to others and it can produce a strong sense of happiness and contentment.

- When you understand what is most important to you, find a way that allows you to live a life being true to this and yourself.

- Everything you do in life counts, everything, every little thing no matter how small.

- When you get it wrong – don't feel bad, give yourself a break and know that learning the lesson is more important.

- Don't give into negativity and feel helpless, take action to make it change, stay solution focused.

- Imagine your life 10 years from now and this will motivate you to do things differently today.

- Reading uplifting books and inspiring biographies helps you to connect to your own dreams and aspirations to make a difference.

- Knowing what you value in life and living those values out daily will make a positive difference to you and those around you.

- Develop your passion in life, no matter what it is or how scared you may feel to express it. Often the thing you fear the most is your heart's deepest desire.

- Finding a way to contribute in some way to other people provides a great sense of gratitude from others and happiness in the knowledge you are doing good.

- Take the time to reflect on what you have achieved in life already.

- Being loving to yourself and others is easy to say, but it produces forgiveness and respect, which is a powerful way to live life filled with purpose.

Recommended reading

Oh, the Places You'll Go! by Dr Seuss
ISBN 978-0679805274

The Happiness Plan by Carmel McConnell
ISBN 978-0273711780

Why talk to a Guru? When you can whisper to a Horse
by Paul Hunting
ISBN 978-1905399147

Feel the Fear and Do It Anyway by Susan Jeffers
ISBN 978-0091907075

Embracing Uncertainty by Susan Jeffers
ISBN 978-0312325831

The Power of Now by Eckhart Tolle
ISBN 978-0340733509

Awaken the Giant Within by Anthony Robbins
ISBN 978-0743409384

Your Best Life Now by Joel Osteen
ISBN 978-0340964514

Introducing NLP Neuro-Linguistic Programming
by Joseph O'Connor & John Seymour
ISBN 978-1855383449

Be Your Own Life Coach: How to Take Control of Your Life and Achieve
Your Wildest Dreams by Fiona Harrold
ISBN 978-0340770641

The Big Book of Me by Nina Grunfeld
ISBN 978-1904977490

The Road Less Travelled by M. Scott Peck
ISBN 978-0099727408

Further Along the Road Less Travelled by M. Scott Peck
ISBN 978-0671015817

The Yellow Book by Richard Wilkins
ISBN 978-0952819813

Living from the Inside Out by Jean-Marie Hamel
ISBN 978-1400052745

My Life Tree by Claus Moller
ISBN 978-8789264707

Getting Things Done: The Art of Stress-Free Productivity
by David Allen
ISBN 978-0142000281

*The Gifts of Imperfection – Let Go of Who You Think You're Supposed to
Be and Embrace Who You Are* by Brené Brown Phd
ISBN 978-1592858491

Transform Your Life: A Blissful Journey by Geshe Kelsang Gyatso
ISBN 978-0948006753

A Long Walk to Freedom: The Autobiography of Nelson Mandela
ISBN 978-0349106533

Reference websites

Here are some interesting websites that have a story behind them and I think you might enjoy learning a little more about…

www.swibonline.com

This is SWIB 'Supporting Women in Business', the professional networking group I founded and began as a little idea I had to help women like myself who had started their own business and needed to meet like-minded women to share support in their local community. It has grown over the years to help women from all walks of life to connect with each other. Women meet in their communities to make friends and learn from each other, so they can collaborate and do what they do best as women – support and encourage one another to be their best in both work and life.

www.uk-smoooth.co.uk

This is a great example of a man who changed his life for what he discovered to be a real passion… He became a teacher of dance and changed his life from being a sales man to something he loves to share and what he believes does make a difference to others. Dave really knows how to help people improve their inner confidence, increase their communication skills and over all well-being through teaching the techniques of modern jive dancing, and at the same time helping his students to overcome their inhibitions. It's just one way you might find some inspiration to improve your own well-being and then find a dance class near you!

www.learnbots.com

My brother Rory left England and went to live in Spain with just $150 in his pocket seeking to make a success of his life, but first he had to master the language! He really struggled to learn the language and after some self-coaching discovered he could learn much faster through visualization and a more creative approach to seeing the language in pictures. He has dedicated his life to making language learning fun and visually entertaining. I am a very proud sister as he turned his life around by following his passion and for all you visual learners, his story and work is inspiring.

www.redbubble.com

My eldest daughter Danni is an artist and introduced me to this great website that supports artists to develop their creativity and the work fills me with inspiration. It's a supportive community for anyone with an interest and values creativity. It's a useful marketplace too, a meeting place and learning place of people, art and writing. So if creativity might be your thing, take a look. I hope you enjoy it.

www.ted.com/speakers/brene_brown.html

This is a website full of inspiring and informative speakers on video. Brene Brown is a fantastic speaker and a professor of social work who studies vulnerability, courage, authenticity and shame. Brene has a ground breaking talk on this site that helps people's awareness of these subjects, she asks how can we learn to embrace our vulnerability.

www.jkrowling.com

J K Rowling is the author of the phenomenal best selling Harry Potter Series. The volume of sales is so high that it has been credited with leading a revival of reading in children. However, what is most inspiring about her, is that she wrote her first book as a single mother, struggling to make ends meet, but is now one of the most successful authors of our day. She never gave up!

A space for your thoughts

....

....

....

....

....

....

....

....

....

....

....

....

....

....

....

....

....

....

Picture credits

Index